AFTER WINTER

Comes

Spring

SONYA P. BRUNDIDGE

SIMPLY   SEASONS   PUBLISHING

After Winter Comes Spring
Copyright © 2006 by Sonya P. Brundidge

Requests for information should be sent to:

Simply Seasons Publishing ©, P.O. Box 4110,
Ft. Eustis, VA 23604;

Unless otherwise noted, all Scripture quotations are from the New King James Version of the Bible. Copyright © 1979, 1980, 1982 by Thomas Nelson, Inc., publishers. Used by permission.

Other Scripture quotations are from the New American Standard Bible, © The Lockman Foundation 1960, 1962, 1963, 1968, 1971, 1972, 1973, 1975, 1977.

All rights reserved. No part of this book may be reproduced in any form, stored in a retrieval system or transmitted in any form by any means---electronic, mechanical, photocopy, recording or otherwise---without prior written permission of the publisher/author, except for brief quotations for review purposes only.

ISBN 978-0-977485-0-1
ISBN 0-9777485-0-2

Cover Design by Sonya P. Brundidge

Printed in the United States of America

ForthWord
(Foreword)

When thinking of a foreword for this book, I had in my heart to have my pastor, Bob Collins, write the foreword. I felt he was the perfect choice because there are few people whom I respect and admire more.

However, I felt God, my Father, saying that He wanted this to be His foreword or "forth word," if you will. I felt impressed that He wanted this book to be my first fruits given back to Him.

Therefore, I unreservedly give God this honor. It was He alone Who spoke to my heart in the still of the night. It was He alone Who gave me words of hope to light my way. And it was He alone Who commissioned me to write words of love to the hearts of many wounded.

When preparing for this book, I told God that I did not want to write a book, but I wanted Him to write a book through me. I asked Him to speak life into each person who would read this book.

So here's to my God, my Father, the Lover of my soul, and my very best Friend. I ask that You send "forth" this "word" from the pages of this book and bring healing and wholeness to everyone who reads it.

Acknowledgments

There is one Whom I owe everything, even my life, and that is God. He is the "I Am" and there is no other besides Him. You have shown me a faithful love like I have never known. I am smitten with You and no one else or nothing else could ever take Your place. You have truly made me feel like royalty. I can hold my head up because of You. You are my world. Be glorified through me. I love You, my Abba. My loyalty is with You.

I could never do acknowledgments and not mention the three people in this world that mean the most to me; my sons. Lawrence, Noah, and Andrew, thank you for being the best sons in the entire universe. We have come through hard times together, but we've had love, laughter, and God all the way. I could never express your great worth in my eyes. You are truly a treasure to my heart. I appreciate your unconditional love, your unyielding support of me, and your undying enthusiasm for working beside me in ministry. You are truly "the three mighty men" of God.

I want to thank you, mom, for who you are in my life. I love you very much and appreciate all that you've ever done for me. You are truly a beautiful person.

I could never grant enough thanks to JoAnn Sampson and ALL the women of "FaithBuilders." You are the best ladies in the world. Thank you so much for loving me, accepting me, and believing in the call of God on my life. I could never forget you.

Such gratitude also goes to my pastor, Bob Collins, who has been an incredible supporter of me and the ministries God has given to me. Thank you for trusting me and giving me so much freedom to grow and be used by God. Thanks for being an example of what a "real man" of God looks like.

I must also thank Mrs. Collins. What an incredible example of a godly woman. Your amazing strength is cloaked by such beauty and grace. Your faith in the midst of adversity deeply inspires me.

Pastor Russell and Sylvia Evenson, "the intercessors," for being examples of true prayer warriors to my sons and me.

And there is my "personal prophetess" Alta Rae Glosson. Thank you for investing in me and believing in my dreams. You're absolutely wonderful. I'm glad you and Roy are in my life.

A special thanks to Marcie Thomas, my dancing sister in Christ, for being willing to help in this project and offer whatever support I needed. How I appreciate your encouragement. I thank God for your friendship and for your listening ear.

Thank you, Kristen Street, for the good times we've shared and the prayer. We've come through some rough times, but just look at what the Lord has done.

Thank you, Gloria Jackson, for your continued encouragement and prayers that I would stay focused and on track. That was no small task. You are truly precious to my heart.

Sandy Phillips, thank you for standing in agreement with me as we prayed over those who would read this book. You are a precious sister in Christ.

Thank you, Patricia, my sister. I am so proud of who you are. I love you very much.

Thank you, Lavorise Love, for watching the boys when I was in such great need. That meant a lot to me. May God repay you.

Thank you, Aminta Colon, my sister, for always being willing to give me a respite to take some time for myself. You're the best!

Thank you, Joe Hanchey, for keeping my machines happy and being a great brother.

Thank you, Merry Dawson, for standing with me and being a friend during some dark moments. Your sincere care meant so much.

And I could never leave out ALL of my friends and family who have been supportive in more ways than I could list. Though I can't list all of you in such limited space, you know who you are. Your prayers and words of encouragement have meant so very much to me. All of you are a great part of who I am.

Dinner Invitation

As I have written this book, I have taken verses of the Bible and wrapped a devotional thought around those verses. However, the chapters surrounding those verses truly bring out the entire fullness of the text. I encourage you to dig deeper and allow the verses I have chosen to whet your appetite for more of God's Word. See my book as only a scrumptious appetizer that tantalizes your spiritual taste buds for more of the rich and meaningful delicacies found in the Bible. Go to these books in the Bible for yourself and read beyond the verses chosen just for that particular devotional.

It is my desire that my book will give you a greater hunger to know God. Taste of His goodness by studying His Words spoken to you. You will see Someone Who loves deeply and you will find yourself deeply loving Him.

God's call to you in Revelations chapter 3, is, "Behold, I stand at the door and knock. If anyone hears My voice and opens the door, I will come in to him and dine with him and he with Me."

Before you read this book, I now extend this dinner invitation to you. You are hereby presented with an opportunity to accept this offer to know Jesus Christ as your very best Friend, your Lord, and Savior of your life. To accept, pray the following prayer aloud:

> Dear Lord Jesus, I accept Your dinner invitation. Please forgive me of my sins and change my whole life around. Jesus, I believe You died for my sins, that You rose from the dead, and that I will live with You eternally. Fill me with Your Holy Spirit and set me free. Give me a passion for others who are lost and a hunger and thirst for what matters most to You. Help me to fulfill all that You've placed me on this earth to do. Now, I thank You that my sins are forgiven, my past is completely washed clean, and I know for certain that I am on my

way to heaven. Help me to dine daily at "Your table" and not that of another. In Jesus Name, Amen.

If you prayed that prayer, please be sure to find a good Bible teaching church to attend and get involved with. Also, make it a habit to pray this prayer with many others. May God bless and keep you. And know that I am praying for you.

***PRAYER REFLECTIONS
AND
NOTES***

Introduction

There was a time in my life when I seriously wondered if the feeling of winter would ever pass. I figured I might just have to settle in for the remaining years ahead because winter was here to stay.

As I was lying on my bed, I cried out to God from the depths of my heart and asked Him if I needed to just get used to this wintry season of life or would spring ever come again. I questioned if I'd ever experience the beauty and new life of springtime or was I to be content with barely existing in the winter of divorce.

That very same day, I went to my mailbox and a local garden shop had sent me a postcard advertising their beautiful bushes and flowers. The front of the postcard had pictures of a variety of spring trees and bushes bursting with color. The only words on the front of the card read, "The Promise of Spring".

In my heart of hearts, I knew that God was directly answering my prayer. He was reassuring me that the season I was in would not last forever. Spring would once again be ushered in on the wings of grace.

I immediately took that postcard and hung it on my bathroom mirror as a reminder of this word of hope from God. I loved the words on that card. Though the words were simple and few, they gently penetrated my heart, as only God could do.

Now let me encourage you with the same encouragement given to me. Though harsh winter winds come and strip the trees bare, the sting of bitter cold lasts only for a season.

God has wondrously revealed to us through His creation that life is ever changing. What comes, passes on; and so the cycle goes.

Winter may boldly take its place on the stage of our lives, but in time it must graciously bow and step aside for
After Winter........

***Comes Spring*!**

PRAYER REFLECTIONS AND NOTES

For behold, the winter is past, the rain is over and gone. The flowers have already appeared in the land.
Song of Solomon 2:11-12a (NASB)

None of this could be true. It happened to other people down the road, down the way. Yet here I was opening the door for the sheriff who was serving me divorce papers. This uniformed officer delivered an envelope to me that would forever change my life. I closed the door behind him, as I slipped into the nearest chair. My heart raced and my hands trembled as my fingers reluctantly removed "the papers" from the envelope.

This was it. What had been only dreadful words was now reality in tangible form. The fact that my marriage was ending in divorce could no longer be denied. Those "other people" who had such things happen to them, suddenly became my children and me.

The sheer terror that struck me was indescribable. I don't know that I had ever felt so out of control in all of my life. The only world that I had known for most of my adult years was collapsing before my eyes. Questions without answers swirled around my head making me feel dizzy and faint.

Emotional pain like I had never experienced before gripped me in the pit of my stomach; a pain that I would not wish on my worst enemy. The agony of that time in my life felt unbearable.

I never thought I would see the day of recovery from that period of life. But as I look back, it seems like so long ago. God has truly healed my heart and restored new life to me.

Though it may be hard for you to believe right now, trust me when I tell you that this season will pass. Given some time, the rain will cease, the clouds will fade, and the flowers of your life will appear once again.

And he arose and came to his father, But when he was still a great way off, his father saw him and had compassion, and ran and fell on his neck and kissed him.   Luke 15:20

The month of November has generally been the month that I dip emotionally. I tend to be an upbeat person without letting much get me down, but if there were a time that I'd be a bit more susceptible to the blues, for whatever reason, November would be the month.

It was a cold November day that I remember seeing the contents of one home divide into two homes. I watched in sheer disbelief, the man who had once been my husband, moving "his" items out of our home. I was grateful that the children were asleep in their rooms and would not have this memory haunting them throughout their lives.

How could this be happening? It seemed like only yesterday we were joining our possessions together, placing them beside each other in perfect harmony. Somehow these possessions knew, as well as I, that things, literally, would never be the same again.

How I dreaded this moment that I knew was coming. How I hated the reality of things never being the same. Sameness and security were what I longed for in a home. And here, even our possessions were trying to inform me that everything was changing. The empty spaces of his belongings being removed from the house echoed throughout the empty spaces of my heart. So much had been stripped away within. I felt so alone, so isolated, and so very weak.

I couldn't handle this on my own, so on a cold November day, I cried out to God for hope, help, and direction. And it was a cold November day that God heard my cry and came running.

If I say "Surely the darkness shall fall on me, even the light shall be night about me; indeed the darkness shall not hide from You. But the night shines as the day; the darkness and the light are both alike to You." Psalm 139:11-12

I remember the initial pain of separation from the one I loved the most. The thought of the permanence of divorce seemed to me unbearable; unthinkable. It was as if I hated having a brain that could actually process the information of what all of this meant. Unfortunately, I was all too aware of what was happening to my marriage, to my family, to my life. I had already peeked into a future of broken dreams, broken promises, and broken hearts. And I did not like what I saw.

The excruciating pain that gripped my heart made me desire death rather than divorce. I longed for the blackness of night to hide my pain. It was as if I could find comfort in a place of darkness that did not force me to see anything. I loved the night. I could pretend in the night. Just as the night covered what my eyes knew to be there; it could also cover all the trouble that my heart knew was there. If only for the night, I could pretend that everything was okay. No one could see my broken world. Even I could act as if all was at peace in the blackness of night. After all, wasn't it at night when people had nightmares that they awakened from? That must be what this was. It was all a bad, bad dream.

I could make myself believe this as long as it was night. But the light of morning would interrupt my denial the way a loud buzzer from an alarm clock abruptly jerks you from a pleasant sleep. Light would reveal all the pain and trouble. Light's tactless honesty would not let me hide from the truth I had to face. My marriage was over and that mountain I was looking at had to be climbed.

I came to the place where I could no longer hide in the night, but had to face the morning. I couldn't keep the blinds closed and pull the covers back over my head acting as if I couldn't see the light. The light was there and I had to once again learn to walk in it, embrace it, and allow it to be my friend and guide.

Jesus, too, is called the Light. He is only Light. There is no darkness found in Him, nor can it remain where He is. The night became light about me as I allowed Jesus to minister to my hurt through His Word. It did take time. It didn't happen over night. It happened by allowing Jesus to walk me through the night. And I can hold out hope to you that, yes, the morning light will once again be a welcomed friend.

PRAYER REFLECTIONS AND NOTES

Strengthen the weak hands, And make firm the feeble knees. Say to those who are fearful-hearted, Be strong, do not fear!
Isaiah 35:3-4a

*F*ear. That gut-renching, spiraling down, feeling that grips you in the pit of your stomach. That helpless and frightening sensation that you are at the utter mercy of something that you have no control over. You frantically reach and feel in the dark for something to hold onto, but there is nothing; nothing but total darkness. That thick blanket of blackness that hides all reason and answer. "Why" cannot be comprehended. "How long" is not yet to be known. All that you know for certain is that you have never been so scared in all of your life. You have never felt so all alone as when the person whom you love walks away. How helpless and hopeless when there is nothing you can say and nothing you can do. "What abouts" are no longer an issue. The die has been cast and the decision has been made without your input and without concern for how it will affect you. The realization that it's over sets in and fear takes its place.

It is precisely at this time that you must quiet your soul and calm your emotions. You must cast off fear because God remains in control even though your life may feel out of control. God knew this would happen and had a plan for you all along. Nothing catches God by surprise. He doesn't need a contingency plan. He just has *A* plan in spite of the contingencies. And His plan will be worked out for us if we completely surrender our lives to Him.

There is no need to fear when you're feeling out of control. You really never were in control in the first place. God was and still is in control. As long as you are holding to His hand, you can be assured that God will lead you through the darkness to a place of brilliant light.

My tears have been my food day and night, while men say to me all day long, "Where is your God?"   *Psalm 42:3*

I remember a time when all I could do was cry. The pain and the helplessness were so intense. I would cry in the morning when I would think of the circumstances I found my life in. I would cry myself to sleep at night somehow hoping my tears would wash away the hurt and sweep me into a gentle lull. I could see no breaking of day and no light at the end of the tunnel. Tears were truly my food during the day and throughout the night.

This passage of Scripture says, "Men say to me all day long, 'Where is your God'?" Truth be known, there were times when I asked myself, "Where is your God?" I could not see His face. I did not feel His presence. And at times, I could not even determine if I was hearing His voice.

I felt so utterly forsaken by the Lord, as well as by man. But it was in this very dark place that I found myself clinging to the God I could not see and looking to Him to spare me. Through my tears I could see a light coming towards me and once upon me, warming me and enfolding me with God's love. This light embraced me, picked me up, and carried me through all the hard places that I encountered.

I did not understand the peace, nor did I have the mental presence to try to figure it all out. All I knew was that God touched me and brushed the tears from my face. He was somehow carrying me through places where my legs would have failed me. His presence cheered me and His light guided me. Whenever I found myself crying again, now I had a Friend who cried with me.

If you find your tears being your food day and night, let the hand of the Master wipe your tears away.

If men come to you and say, "Where is your God?" you can confidently say, "Don't you see Him? He is the One Who is carrying me with tears in His eyes."

PRAYER REFLECTIONS AND NOTES

For I know the plans I have for you," declares the Lord, "plans to prosper you and not to harm you, plans to give you hope and a future." Jeremiah 29:11

These were words I really needed to hear when I was first separated and even more so as the entire divorce process unfolded. I somehow felt that because I was going through a divorce, God had no use for me anymore. I would have to be put on the shelf with the "washed up" ones. I had been "benched" due to injury. I felt that I was no longer picture perfect and therefore not useful for the kingdom of God.

The grief and the shame made me feel like an ostrich wanting to bury its head in the sand. I felt like one of the ones who had failed God and had to return to the damaged goods' box. I could not see a bright future even on the clearest of days. I thought within myself, "What kind of good witness could I possibly be as a divorced woman in the church? What could I even say to someone who was searching for God or in need of His guidance? I figured I might as well face it and realize that I would have no part with those "whole Christians" who were not a part of the "broken body".

And then I read Jeremiah 29:11. Just to know that God truly had a plan for my life and saw me as a valuable vessel was beyond my comprehension. God said to me that He had plans to give me hope where I felt hopeless. He wanted to give me a future when I could barely see into the next hour. My Father wanted to prosper little old me. He was not concerned with what others were looking at as a failure. God was only seeing what He knew my life was always meant to be.

Know that He has BIG, wonderful plans for your life. Life for you isn't over. This is just the beginning of another chapter in your life on your journey with God. So do not feel ashamed or like you have failed. God holds your tear-stained face in His hands and kisses your tears away. He whispers in your ear that everything is going to be all right. Just as you were beginning to think that He was punishing you with all of this pain, He caresses you and says that He does not want to harm you, but to prosper you. Trust Him and know that. Dare to believe that. And watch the Father's plans for your life unfold.

PRAYER REFLECTIONS AND NOTES

Do not hide your face from me, do not turn your servant away in anger; you have been my helper. Do not reject me or forsake me, O God my Savior. Though my father and mother forsake me, the Lord will receive me.
Psalm 27:9-10

Often times in divorce you have one person who wanted the divorce and the other who did not. In the case where you are the party who did not want the divorce, rejection often sets in. You may see yourself as better off without this person in your life, but that feeling of knowing that you wanted to work something out and someone else didn't can cause deep feelings of rejection like nothing you've ever experienced.

It can be very difficult to understand someone taking your years of investment into the relationship and casually casting them aside as if they were mere debris in the wind. It can be very disillusioning to see all of your future hopes and dreams shattered at the hand of the one you trusted most.

The words, "I don't love you anymore" are etched in stone in your mind and you can never forget the place and time that you heard them. You believe this pain will never go away and yet when you look into the face of God, you see Someone Who will never leave you nor forsake you. You see Someone Who deems you valuable and precious beyond measure.

A father and even a mother may forsake you, but you have a God Who will NEVER forsake you. At your best and at your worst; no need to worry. You have permanent security in Him. Do not devalue your personhood at the unkind hand of another. See yourself as God sees you. He sees you as wonderful, lovely, and to be cherished and adored.

As you timidly walk toward Him, desiring His arms to warmly embrace you, let this passage of Scripture assure you that "the Lord WILL receive you." So run, child, into the arms of Him Who will never turn you away.

But You, O Lord, are a shield for me; my glory and the lifter of my head.
Psalm 3:3

*H*ere I was, all of a sudden, alone with three small children. I felt embarrassed and humiliated. I felt a need to explain myself and who we were to others. Didn't they at least deserve to know that I was once happily married, or so I thought.

I felt self-conscious and thought everyone was noticing that we were not accompanied by an adult male figure.

I would sometimes go out and see women with just their children and find a little comfort in knowing that I was not the only one in the world having to go it alone. Then, up from behind, would come their spouse who would kiss them and playfully toss the children in the air. I would feel the silent camaraderie that we had shared, slip into that place where I put all my other imaginations stifled by reality.

How could I possibly stand on my own, all alone, and be strong for these little boys whom God had blessed me with? Could a woman actually be seen as significant in the eyes of the world if she was flying solo? I didn't know for sure. I would find myself being apologetic to the world that I had somehow failed. I hung my head and avoided eye contact many a time. I felt too small and too shattered to walk with confidence. All I could do was walk, for if I didn't walk, my children nor I would get to the other side, wherever that might be.

I took my insecurity, my embarrassment, and shame and said, "Here, God. Please take this and do something with it. I don't want it anymore." And He did. He looked at me and told me that HE was my glory and the lifter of my head. Wow, He would be my glory.

He placed a gentle finger under my chin, raised my head up, and deeply looked into my soul, as if to say, "You're with me now and it's going to be all right. You are somebody and just look at Whom you're walking with." In time, the realization of Who was with me, caused me to walk with a head held higher than most women whom I knew, married or not.

Yes, a human hand can lift you, but only for so long. But when you allow God to be your glory and the Lifter of your head, it is then that you will know a confidence and a security that nothing or no one can ever erase.

*PRAYER REFLECTIONS
AND
NOTES*

Again, if two lie down together, they will keep warm. But how can one be warm alone? Though one may be overpowered by another, two can withstand him. And a three-fold cord is not quickly broken. Ecclesiastes 4:11-12

I think one of the most difficult things about being divorced is that whenever trials come into my life or problems come along, it can feel so lonely at those times. I can feel so isolated and oh, so alone. There is that disquieting feeling we experience when we have to weather the storm all alone. There is no one there to physically hold us in their arms until the rough weather passes on. There is no one to tell us in the still and quiet of the night, that it is going to be all right. Who is there beside us in the bed whom we can awaken in the night and ask them to pull us close? Who wraps their arms around us so that we feel safe and secure?

It is at these times that I can feel the pain of being "one" instead of being "two." Since I usually solve my problems by talking to someone and bouncing ideas off of them, I feel the impact of divorce in this way the most. The Bible tells us that if two lie down together they keep warm, but how can one be warm alone?" How chilly it feels when the winter breezes of life blow and there is just you alone to deal with the elements.

But just about the time that I feel all alone in the midst of my circumstances, the Father, Himself, reminds me that I am never, ever alone. It doesn't matter whether I've been good or bad. Whether I was wronged or it was at my hand that the wrong took place. The Father is still there beside me to love me and to hold me. He never leaves me to handle the troubles of this life all alone.

Yes, two are truly better than one, especially when God makes up one of the two. For if you fall, it is God, Himself, Who will lift you up. When you lie down, it will be God Who will keep you warm. You must never fear that you will be overpowered as one who stands alone. God will give you the ability to resist. It will be in Him that you will triumph. When God makes up any part of your strand, you can rest assured that you WILL NOT be torn apart.

PRAYER REFLECTIONS AND NOTES

Then they all forsook Jesus and fled.
Mark 14:50

I cannot even imagine exactly what that must have felt like to Jesus. I can empathize with Jesus to a point, but He must have felt utterly forsaken by humanity. The humanity He had helped. The humanity He had held in His heart. What it must have been like to have people needing you and wanting you all the time. Crowds hanging on your every word. Wherever you went, a multitude would follow. The only solitude that you could get was that which you took in the early hours of the morning.

Jesus was surrounded by people much of the time. As long as He had something to give, the people were innumerable. But then, as soon as He was in a troublesome predicament, all of the people left Him totally alone. Even His disciples left Him alone.

Isn't that how you felt during divorce? Everyone's situation is different, but anyone who is separated or divorced has had moments of aloneness. My moments were very severe. Most of my close friends and neighbors had moved away at the same time. My family was out of state and really didn't know or understand how to reach out to me. My husband and I had started looking for another church just before the separation, so I didn't have support from fellow Christians. All the remaining friends I had were mutual friends that we met when we moved to the area. And since these mutual friends didn't want to "choose sides," they just left me bleeding beside the curb. However, some did wish me well before they drove off.

You might also be feeling destitute and alone, just as I felt. But I learned that Jesus really is all we need, when He's all we have. I began to fervently pray to God and read His Words in the Bible. I found such peace, comfort, joy, love, and acceptance in those pages.

Even though, "they all left me and fled," God's truth stood beside me like a faithful and constant companion. His truth will stand beside you, as well.

PRAYER REFLECTIONS AND NOTES

For I will restore health to you and heal you of your wounds, says the Lord. Because they called you an outcast saying, "This is Zion. No one wants her." Jeremiah. 30:17

A divorce can leave you feeling just like this passage of Scripture states; that no one wants you. Your heart is wounded and your self-worth is bruised. Many words have been spoken to you that cause you to think that no one could ever love you and no one would ever want you again. You see the shattered pieces of your life lying all around you. You can't imagine the puzzle ever being fitted together again. To hope that you'll ever love or be loved again is to think the impossible.

Yet, nothing is too difficult for God. He not only can restore your emotional health; He will restore it. Though you may feel like you've fallen too far, God can place you back on the saddle of life again. People may have mocked you to your face and counted you out of the race, but God said it wasn't over for you. He has the power to bring you out of captivity and into a place of freedom. He has a way of turning the tables in your favor. About the time that you are knocked out and the count is up to nine, God gives you the strength to stand to your feet once again.

Don't focus your attention on yourself, your past, and all that was. But realize that the Creator of all the beauty of the world, loves and wants you. You still have beauty and worth and yes, you are desirable.

For your Maker is your husband. The Lord of hosts is His name; And your Redeemer is the Holy One of Israel; He is called the God of the whole earth. For the Lord has called you; Like a woman forsaken and grieved in spirit, Like a youthful wife when you were refused," Says your God.   Isaiah 54:5-6

I liken marriage to a journey. Once you start your life on your own and leave your parents, you discover that this journey of life can be very lonely at times. So you begin to consider with whom you wish to make this journey. You give careful consideration to what kind of person you would like to travel with on this life-long journey. You pray about it, you consult others about it, and you make your choice of who will be your partner.

The decision is made, family and friends are notified, and the journey of two begins. You realize that the journey will be difficult at times and hilariously joyful at others. But you feel confident that the person you have chosen will help you successfully navigate through this journey. This chosen partner will know how to help you survive the steepest parts of the mountain and the most dangerous paths on the road of life. This chosen partner will lighten the load and administer aid when you need it. When you are down or just not at your best, this one will never forsake you. You're in this thing for life. You feel you have no need to worry because the partner you have chosen will be there through thick and thin, loyal 'til death. Somehow you rest a little bit easier knowing that in a world of ups and down and ins and outs, you at least have this one person who will remain constant and will weather the storms of life with you.

And then, one day, all of that changes. Your partner decides that he or she does not wish to make the journey with you. They say, "Thank you for your help in getting me to this point, but your services will no longer be needed by me for the rest of my journey. I have chosen another to take up where you left off and I feel that they will suit my purposes from this point forward much better than you. Goodbye."

The forsaken partner is suddenly in quite a predicament. He or she can do nothing to change the other person's mind and must swallow this bitter pill of reality. You are no longer loved by this person. You are no longer wanted by this person. Years have gone by, energy has been expended, and you are merely left with missing pages from a book. Pages that you both had ever so carefully written together in your great book of life. Abruptly, your partner tears a large portion of the book away from the binding.

You are left to try to figure out what you should salvage and what you are to completely discard. You ask yourself questions such as, "Am I to finish the journey alone or am I to find another partner to help me on my journey? And if I do find someone whom I feel is capable of walking this journey with me, can I really trust my own judgment again? After all, didn't I make a horrible mistake with the first choice? What if this person damages the pages of the book even worse than the first partner?"

It all becomes so complicated within your mind. It is a decision you should have never been forced to make. It was never a part of God's plan for a person to decide if and when they would change partners. With this covenant, only death would constitute a need for a new partner. Since God is He Who decides when we are to exit this earth and what we are to do while we are in it, it is His choice when it is time for a change in partners.

Nevertheless, because of the fallen condition of man, alternate plans have had to be introduced into the entire scheme of things.

No, our journey need not be one that we make alone. As long as we shall live, we have a partner for the journey. One Who knows the way because He is the way. One in Whom we can completely trust; even blindly trust. He is the best Partner anyone could ever have.

I invite you, today, to make Christ your Partner for life. He will help you rewrite every lost page of the book.

Even if you should choose another partner for your journey, never let go of Christ. For it is with Christ that you will never walk alone again.

*PRAYER REFLECTIONS
AND
NOTES*

The people asked, and God brought quail and satisfied them with the bread of heaven.
Psalm 105:40

I recently heard someone talk about a poll taken by Gallup. They asked Americans what irritated them the most. The number one answer on the list was not getting what they paid for; not acquiring what they had invested in. When I heard that, I absolutely agreed.

It takes me a long time to do my research, cost compare, and ask a few people their opinions about a product before I finally break down and buy it. I will look in the Consumer Report. I spend time in prayer. And I usually put the purchase off until I can truly justify the need beyond the desire for it. This attitude really helps to keep me out of financial trouble and has also spared me a great deal of pain and regret. Doing my homework has often paid off.

However, there have been those occasions when I bought something and was duped.

I remember the time when I bought a used washer. It looked practically new on the outside. The elderly lady who was selling it said that she had barely used it and only set it out in the garage because she moved to her present home.

I was delighted with this great deal and quickly installed it so that I could wash the mountain of dirty laundry that had accumulated. I placed the first load of laundry in. Everything worked beautifully. When I returned to the kitchen to remove the clothes, I was horrified. There was water everywhere. I was grabbing towels, rags, and anything I could get my hands on to clean up the mess. I was in tears.

I called this lady on the phone and let her know that she could choose to give me my check back or I could cancel it. Either way, I was not paying for something that didn't work. I had definitely not gotten what I had paid for.

This was exactly how I felt with my marriage. Marriage had seemed to promise so much. It had looked great on the outside, but in the end, I was in tears trying to grab at anything to clean up the mess. I had made such an investment in marriage; emotionally, mentally, physically, and spiritually. When it didn't work like I had expected, I felt like those irritated Americans polled by Gallup. I didn't get what I paid for. My heart felt empty and I couldn't get any of my investment back. I gave it all.

What I had to do was to take my spent life and cash it in to Jesus. I knew that was the only way I could redeem anything from all that was lost.

Perhaps, you are also feeling like the people in that Gallup poll. But do as I did. Give your empty heart to Jesus. You will be far from irritated. You will see that with Jesus, you will get not only what you paid for, but so much more. He never leaves a customer unsatisfied.

PRAYER REFLECTIONS
AND
NOTES

Jehoshaphat made merchant ships to go to Ophir for gold, but they never sailed, for the ships were wrecked at Ezion Geber.
1 Kings 22:48

When I was a child, I loved the song, "Somewhere Over the Rainbow." It was so wonderful for my juvenile mind to imagine a place where all ended well. A place where all wrongs became right and all bad became good. I was so idealistic and I had grandiose expectations of what life should be like. I was intelligent and realistic enough to know that my childhood wasn't all that it should be, but I just figured once I became an adult, I could get to that other side of the rainbow. I would build my ship in life and set sail for that pot of gold at the end of the rainbow.

We all have had secret hopes and dreams. We have all built ships from various materials of life. The material might be education. It might be relationships, careers, or anything that we thought would transport us to our pot of gold. And just what might that pot of gold be? It could be anything that you thought would result in your happiness at the end of the journey.

Most people make decisions that they think will result in them receiving joy. Marriage is surely one such decision. But we often find ourselves in Jehoshaphat's predicament. We have made ships to set off for gold, but they never sailed. They were shipwrecked.

Of all decisions that we make in life, outside of following Christ, marriage is the one ship that we put all of our hopes and trust in. We really believe this ship of marriage is going to bring us lasting love and a lifetime of joy. We believe we will have a treasure of family memories that we will carry with us forever. Then these dreams and hopes are dashed against the rocks of divorce.
What do you do when your ship has been wrecked? I turned to God with all those broken pieces about me. I cried out to Him to help me; to save me. I asked God to show me true happiness, joy, and peace. I found that peace in the

pages of His Word and by seeking Him and His plan for my life.

My expectation is now in God and what He has for me and not in someone else. I desire to please Him with my life. I am amazed at the joy I experience with that focus.

Yes, there is a pot of gold for you at the end of the rainbow; just make sure you set sail in the right ship.

***PRAYER REFLECTIONS
AND
NOTES***

Now it happened after these things that the son of the woman who owned the house became sick. And his sickness was so serious that there was no breath left in him. So she said to Elijah, "What have I to do with you, O man of God? Have you come to me to bring my sin to remembrance, and to kill my son?" And he said to her, "Give me your son." So he took him out of her arms and carried him to the upper room where he was staying, and laid him on his own bed.
1 Kings 17:17-19

*T*his widow woman had only one thing of great value to her. That was her son. Her husband was old in age and there would be no other children. Her son was all that she had. This son was her hope for the future. She would raise him and provide for him, but in her old age, he would provide for her.

Through this son, her bloodline would continue and the name of the family would go on. This son symbolized destiny. Every day that she saw him awake from his sleep, it gave her reason to live; reason to rejoice; reason to believe.

But here he was sick. He had actually died, but she could not even bring herself to face that fact. She was in denial to the fact that her son had no breath left in him. She could not let go. So when she finally came in contact with God via Elijah, she says, "I don't want anything to do with you, O man of God. Have you come to remind me of everything I've ever done wrong and then as punishment take my son's life?" And he said to her, "Give me your son."

As this son was to the widow, was your marriage your one prized possession? Was your spouse your hope, your future, your life? Had you gained your value and significance from being married? Have you found yourself saying to God exactly what the widow woman said to Him? "I don't want anything to do with you. I've tried to serve you and to do what's right. I have done some wrong things, but you know I have tried. Now, God, do you want to remind me of all my faults and sins as reason for my failing marriage?"

We sometimes see God as the mean judge who is just waiting to slam us with the law. Yet, He says to you, as Elijah said to the widow woman; "Give me you son."

Give God your failed relationship, your life, your hopes, your dreams, your everything. Give Him your one and only prized possession. God doesn't want to slam you. He wants to bring life to those things that have died and left you feeling helpless. God wants to show you how He can love you like no other. God wants to show you just how much you mean to Him. He's not here to do an inventory of your past wrongs.

What the woman got in the end was a son who lived; a hope restored. God chooses to restore our hope in different ways. But just trust Him. Give Him "your son" and marvel at how He restores new life to you.

PRAYER REFLECTIONS AND NOTES

Thus says the Lord: "A voice was heard in Ramah; lamentation and bitter weeping. Rachel weeping for her children; refusing to be comforted for her children because they are no more." Jeremiah 31:15

You conceive them. You nurture them. You feel them growing within your womb. Their every movement is a part of you. There is no part of your world, your life, your existence that is separate from them for the entirety of nine months. There is a bond that has been forged from this kind of intimacy that can never be duplicated nor divided. They are a part of your life always. You deliver them into this world, but the umbilical cord to your heart is never cut.

You bring them into the world and meet this one whom you have grown to love. Their beauty is indescribable. The love you felt for them while they were within you is now intensified beyond description. You nurse them, you feed them, you care for them even if your needs go unmet. The love is sacrificial like no other. The love of a mother for her child cannot be described in mere human language. So when I think of what hurts the most in a divorce, it would have to be the loss of your children or the threat of losing them. To have someone even breathe a hint of this is more painful than anyone can comprehend.

Such a thought is unthinkable when one marries and has a child with the one whom they love. So to have this become a part of all the other emotional upheaval that one experiences during this time is enough to cause you to feel a pain you have never known; a pain that goes even deeper than the divorce itself. One loss is unbearable; the other unthinkable. Loss upon loss. Grief upon grief. When will I see you again is a question that no one wants to be faced with concerning his or her child.

Though I have danced in the shadows of such dilemma, I have known those who have had to live out this nightmare day after day.

I give no pat and dry answers to anyone who has gone through this or who is living it out now. What I do say to you is to continue to believe God to work this out for your good and for His glory. When it is all said and done, you will see His great deliverance in your behalf. You will see how so much good came from a situation that you thought would kill you. But continue to trust God and don't give up. He loves you and He sees your pain. When it hurts too bad to even feel anything anymore, just press into God and allow yourself to be loved by the One who never forsakes nor abandons. And though I am so far away from you, I do care for you and I am praying for you with love.

PRAYER REFLECTIONS AND NOTES

And she answered, "This woman said to me 'Give your son, that we may eat him today, and we will eat my son tomorrow.' So we boiled my son, and ate him. And I said to her on the next day, "give your son, that we may eat him; but she has hidden her son."
2 Kings 6:27b-29

Perhaps you may be feeling like giving up on everything in your life right now and maybe even giving up on life itself. The disillusionment of divorce can leave you in a state of despair. There are so many decisions to make, and so many questions that seem to have no answers. You might believe that there is absolutely no way out of this mess which leads you to conclude that there is no hope for your tomorrow.

The woman in this passage of Scripture felt very hopeless. She was hopeless to the point of consuming her offspring; the offspring that was her future. By doing this, she cut off her hope of a future. She saw no other way out of her utter despair and emptiness.

In her desperation to survive, she did the unthinkable.

But what would have happened had she held on for just one more day? The Bible tells us that the windows of heaven opened up for her and her people. Had she held onto hope one day longer, she would have seen how God could make a way where there seemed to be no way. She would have had all the provisions she could have handled. She would still have the life of her child if only she had the faith to believe in the power of just one more day.

What is impossible in one day with man is no difficult thing for the Lord. No matter how bleak your future may appear, I encourage you to entrust your tomorrow to God.

In my own life, I felt like giving up, but God encouraged me to keep on persevering. What looked like utter ruin, God somehow restored.

I am so happy that I didn't give up on God even when I felt like giving up on myself and my situation. Don't you give up either. Though things may look as if there is no way out, trust in the

God Who can show you the power of just one more day.

PRAYER REFLECTIONS AND NOTES

So the King appointed a certain officer for her saying, "Restore all that was hers and all the proceeds of the field from the day that she left the land until now." 2 Kings 8:6

I can remember the day that my ex-spouse moved out of our home. I remember the things that he took and the things that I kept. I also remember the movers coming and dividing what would stay with me and what would go with him. I left that home feeling stripped of so much. I felt ravaged emotionally, physically, spiritually, and financially. I could not even fathom a day of feeling whole or complete again. Would I ever get back on my feet again? Would I ever be able to fully function again? It was so difficult for me at that time. I felt like a refugee having to leave behind what I had always known, only to go to make a new home in an unknown land. That is really how it felt. It was rough. But praise be to God, the day came when I began to feel restoration taking place. I still feel that I am being restored.

This Shunamite woman had to leave her home in a hurry and did not come back for seven years. She didn't want to leave. She had to leave. She had to leave everything that she had ever known. She uprooted her family and dwelt in an unfamiliar land.

After seven years of being gone, it was time for her to make a comeback. She made an appeal to the king for her house and for her land. This king had not been known for his mercy or justice, but with this godly woman, he ordered that her house and land be restored. He also ordered that all of the interest accrued on her land from the time that she had moved away be totally restored.

That's what God desires to do for you. God is a restoring God. Your miracle of restoration might come in a different way. But I believe with all my heart that however God chooses to restore, when He restores, you WILL get back more than you ever had before.

Can a mother forget the baby at her breast and have no compassion on the child she has borne? Though a mother may forget, I will not forget!"   Isaiah 49:15

*H*ave you ever felt forgotten? Have you ever had people come up to you or to someone else you know who is divorced and say things like, "that ex of yours will really come to see what a mistake he made one day." "He will really regret what he lost in you." I used to feel like saying, "Yeah, yeah, whatever. He is probably having the time of his life and has chosen to forget any and all good that we once shared with each other." I felt forgotten by him and I felt forgotten by friends and family.

There seems to be that time during a divorce when you really expect time to stand still for you. You feel that time actually owes you that much. You are hurting and your world has just been thrown into complete pandemonium. You soon realize, however, that time has beheld the most heartrending of events throughout all of history and has not for the least nor the greatest, ever stopped its ordained mission. And you and I fall into the category of "heartrending events throughout all of history" that time just won't stop for.

And as far as family and friends go, well, their lives must continue on, too. They would love to stop for a spell and commiserate with you, but their lives are filled with responsibilities and cares of their own. You know that they care, but at times it seems they have completely forgotten about what you feel on the inside. And realistically, no one can walk the path with you both day and night as you journey through the course of a divorce.

That is, no one, but God. He says in Isaiah that though a mother may forget the child that she once nursed at her breast, I WILL NOT forget you. Doesn't that just bless your very soul. God will not forget you.

Time, family, friends, and yes, the person whom you once shared all of your hopes and dreams with, may forget you, but GOD WILL NOT. GOD CANNOT. Isn't that something to think on?

So now when you think of something that God cannot do, you will know that forgetting about you is one of them.

PRAYER REFLECTIONS AND NOTES

If we confess our sins, He is faithful and just to forgive us our sins and to cleanse us from all unrighteousness.   I John 1:9

One thing that satan will try to do to a separated or divorced person is to fill them with guilt. Some people have many things that they know they have done wrong to contribute to the dissolution of the marriage. Other people did everything they could to make the marriage successful and their marriage partner didn't do much to keep it together. However, the partner who tried still feels an extreme amount of guilt because the marriage didn't work. Somehow satan has succeeded at making this person feel like a failure, not only at marriage, but a failure in life.

satan will try to get you to focus on all the wrong things you ever did or ever said in the marriage. He will try to blind you to any of your positive contributions or any of the many right things you did that made you a wonderful person to begin with. Don't allow satan to keep you in this mentally and emotionally defeating cycle.

    Here's what you do; realize that, yes, you are human, therefore you did make some mistakes. Now take some time to confess those mistakes to God. Know that God has just heard you and He is faithful and just to forgive you of your past mistakes and will cleanse you from ALL, not just some, but all of your unrighteousness. Now by faith, walk in squeaky clean freedom and don't wallow in the mud of regret any longer.

Woman, where are those accusers of yours? Has no one condemned you? She said, "No one, Lord. "And Jesus said to her, "Neither do I condemn you; Now go and sin no more."   John 8:10-11

Faults are like hairs. We may be born with few, but before it's all said and done, they're everywhere. We all have them.

Often I have been perplexed at how one human being can boisterously accuse another human being of a fault which they, themselves, have been overtaken with.

I remember when some people found out that I was separated. They treated me with a measure of contempt. Some of these people had previously come to me with serious marital issues they were having. Some of these marriages were hanging on by a thread. Now, here they were glaring at my situation with accusing eyes instead of sympathy.

In Bible days, things weren't much different. Some religious men brought a woman to Jesus who had been caught in the act of sin. They were ready to tear this woman to shreds and stone her to death for this horrible crime of adultery. But I have always loved Jesus' kind and loving approach in this situation.

Here He was, perfect in every way. He had a right to come down hard on this less than holy woman. But Jesus didn't do that. He dealt with her accusers. He forced the accusers to look at their own lives and to determine if they still wanted to have a "rock concert." By the time Jesus rather quietly dealt with each of them, the "rock band" decided to cancel their performance. Jesus looked at her and asked, "Woman, where are those accusers of yours? Has no one condemned you?" She said, "No one, Lord." Jesus said, "Neither do I condemn you. Now, go and sin no more."

There is really nothing I can add to this most beautiful depiction of Christ's mercy and grace. All I can say is that whenever someone comes to accuse you, and they will come, remember how Jesus handled this situation. Be aware that all have sinned and come short of the glory of God, but when you go before God in humility, He will forgive your sin. His only requirement is that you go and sin no more. He doesn't put you on parole. He doesn't condemn you. Tell me, now, if He does not condemn you, who else can?

PRAYER REFLECTIONS
AND
NOTES

We saw the anguish of his soul when he pleaded with us, and we would not hear;......Genesis 42:21a

I have been reading through the book of Genesis lately. I just read some verses describing what Joseph, the son of Jacob, felt like when his brothers put him down into the pit.

I had read the story before, but I hadn't remembered what he had done after they put him in there. I wondered if he was just so spiritual that he was down there singing "praises in the pit." But this verse tells us exactly what he did. He begged. He pleaded with them not to do this evil thing. They looked upon his face, filled with horror and anguish, and they walked away and left him there regardless of his pleading. Wow! What a picture of divorce if you were the person left behind.

I tried to do anything to keep my ex-husband from ripping our family apart. I didn't want us to be another statistic of a marriage ending in divorce. I showed him Bible verses of where it was not God's best and how much God hated divorce. I asked him what I could do differently and I would do it, even though I knew that it was he who had transgressed. All I knew was that I didn't want my marriage or my family to be thrown into a pit. I felt so desperate in my heart and soul. I called ministries for prayer. I listened to whatever inspiration I could find for hope and strength. I was in great need of help. I could see that my ex-husband was going to do this thing regardless of how I pleaded. He even said that if God handed me to him perfect, on a silver platter, he didn't want me anymore. Can you imagine the pit that I was cast into at that moment? The realization finally hit me that I could do whatever it took. This person could see the anguish of my soul as I pleaded, yet "he was not going to hear."

But praise be to God, the story ended well for Joseph and the story ended well for me. And you better believe that it can also end well for you. The pit was just a steppingstone to the great and wonderful things ahead for Joseph. Sometimes in life, things seem so horrible and we feel that we will never get over them. Yet, when we trace over the hand of God, and follow the stream of our lives, we will see how God used those valleys to lead us to the mountaintops. In time, we will look back over our lives and be grateful for all that we went through. We will see how God, if we allowed, turned something so painful into something so positive.

We might have been placed in the pit against our own will, but it becomes our choice whether or not we stay there.

PRAYER REFLECTIONS
AND
NOTES

But he himself (Elijah) went a day's journey into the wilderness, and came and sat down under a broom tree. And he prayed that he might die and said, "It is enough! Now, Lord, take my life for I am no better than my fathers!" (who are already dead).
1 Kings 19:4

Can you not relate to this passage? My divorce seemed to last much longer than other people's divorces. I was always in court and then working on the next court date for a period of about three years. It was not a pleasant experience. I represented myself in court and had no legal experience prior to my divorce, so I did a great deal of research on my own. Lawyers didn't want to help me and friends didn't understand why I was doing what I was doing. All I knew was that I believed God wanted me to do it this way.

Because I was unrepresented by a lawyer, the judge and my ex-husband's lawyer really took me through the wringer. They did things to me that I am assured they would have never done to another lawyer. The lawyer and the judge belittled me and ridiculed me during much of the process. I was handling all of the legal procedures, handling my own heartbreak, handling the emotions of my children, and trying to maintain the day-to-day stuff called life.

There were times I felt exactly like Elijah. As a matter of fact, I remember feeling just that way when I came across this story in the Bible. I had just said to God that I had had enough! I told Him that life was just too hard and I did not know how to run the race anymore. I wanted to stop feeling the pain. I wanted to stop litigating with the man I had married, had trusted, and loved. I wanted out!

But God never let me give up. I had to fight on all points. I had to learn that if I kept on stepping, I would get to the other side. I learned to trust God and to keep walking.

Much of that time seems like a bad dream that someone awakened me from. But at that particular time in my life, there were days when all I wanted to do was find out where the checkout line was.

Let me encourage you to trust God and to keep walking. No matter how dark it becomes, no matter how tired you feel, please keep on trustin' and keep on truckin.' You will eventually make it to the other side.

PRAYER REFLECTIONS AND NOTES

Now as Peter was below in the courtyard, one of the servant girls of the high priest came. And when she saw Peter warming himself, she looked at him and said, "You also were with Jesus of Nazareth." But he denied it, saying, "I neither know nor understand what you are saying." And he went out on the porch, and a rooster crowed.   Mark 14:66-68

I like many things about myself, but there are a few things I could stand to improve upon. One of them is feeling a need to explain myself or my actions to others. I have seen God gradually working this kink out of my life because it's not of Him.

Peter, too, must have struggled with this compulsion. Mark Chapter 14 tells us that one of the servant girls of the high priest came. She looked at Peter while he was warming himself by the fire and she simply said, "You also were with Jesus of Nazareth." This accuser was only a child who was just a servant. Peter owed her neither response nor any explanation. She possessed no authority to do anything one way or the other. Yet, Peter felt a need to explain himself to her.

We can strongly feel this need during a separation or a divorce. When you find yourself trying to gain some warmth and comfort by the fireside, "servant girls" will appear out of nowhere. People you didn't even realize knew you will come to you with questions which are of none of their concern.

I had people who hadn't called me in years trying to find out my side of the story. In a few desperate attempts to rally whatever support I could, I released information that I should have kept to myself. It was an attempt on my part to clarify the situation. But the vast majority of people didn't want clarity. They wanted a few more parts and pieces to add to their own concoction.

Save yourself the frustration, disappointment, and heartache of unnecessary explanation. Simply remain silent. You owe no one an explanation for what you are or who you are.

During the most difficult times of your life when you are comforting yourself by the fire, be assured that "servant girls" will come. But listen to me when I tell you, you owe them nothing. Be willing to let them believe what they want to believe. Nothing you say will change their preconceptions anyway. God knowing you and you knowing God, is all that really matters.

***PRAYER REFLECTIONS
AND
NOTES***

And the scribes and the Pharisees were watching Him closely, to see if He healed on the Sabbath, in order that they might find reason to accuse Him.   Luke 6:7 (NASB)

There is one thing that you must know as a divorced person. It is the fact that others will look for reasons to pass judgment on you or to accuse you. People whom you thought were friends and those who don't know you at all will both have their judgmental views as to what really happened in your situation. They will craftily construct bits and pieces of information that they have observed. Then they will put together small sound bytes of what they have heard. What they will come up with next is their form of what happened in the breakdown of your relationship with an exact measurement of where the fault lies.

When you get right down to it, either people want to help you or they don't, regardless of where the blame lines fall. You could give them the most accurate account of what happened that you could possibly muster, and whoever wanted to accuse you, still would accuse you. It is absolutely not worth your energy.

The best thing to do with your life during a separation, divorce, and afterwards is to simply live it the best way you know how to before God. What others say and think, matters not. There are those Pharisees in life who are looking to accuse you and detract from whatever you do or say, no matter how good it is.

There will always be critics in life. Don't live your life trying to defend yourself from their criticisms. Truth always stands no matter what. While critics and their judgments will fade, truth will always expose itself.

You must learn to cherish the truth that you possess concerning yourself and your situation. You must treasure the fleeting gift God gave you called "the present." Yesterday is a chapter closed. If others want to waste their time reading it over and over again, just let them. But you thank God for giving you another chance to live a whole and happy life with the people whom you love and who love you. After all, there will always be those who are looking for a reason to accuse.

PRAYER REFLECTIONS AND NOTES

If Your sons have sinned against God, He has cast them away for their transgression. If you would earnestly seek God and make your supplication to the Almighty; If you were pure and upright, surely now, He would awake for you and prosper your rightful dwelling place.   Job 8:4-6

*H*ere Job sits in utter despondency. He has lost everything, even his beloved children. He was stripped of what he had loved the most.

Job was what you would have called a real family man. He had one of those families that you see posing for holiday magazines. All the family, all the friends, and even the neighbors are invited to partake in the holiday festivities. Everything is replete with decorations and all the trimmings.

But Job's family didn't end their feasting after the holidays. His children would continue feasting from house to house with each other. All the siblings loved being with one another as often as they could. Job loved his children so much that he would sanctify them after every get together. He would also rise early in the morning and pray on behalf of every single one of them. He was concerned about their hearts and attitudes toward God.

Wow! Who could compare to this man? Yet when Job lost his beloved children to what we would now call a natural disaster, Job's friends did not offer much comfort or consolation to him. They believed that his predicament was what he deserved. He was only getting what he had coming to him.

Here Job was, grieving the death of not one, but all of his children, and the only comforting words his friends could come up with were, "Your children have been killed by God because they apparently sinned against Him." Shouldn't that go on a Hallmark bereavement card?

Yet, I have found that "friends" haven't changed much since Job's day. People said the most insensitive things to me when I was at my lowest point. I felt so grieved and destitute in my heart.

My head would lift in hope and expectancy as I would see a friend coming. Unfortunately, most of those who did come, only came as judges assessing how the blame should be properly allocated. The arrogance and audacity of people stunned me, but I soon got used to it as it came more often than not.

Job learned, as I came to learn, that we don't always know why things happen, but we can always trust in the grace and lovingkindness of our God.

God did require Job to forgive his "wrongly accusing" friends. But after that, God blessed Job's latter life much more than anything he had known before.

Have hope in knowing that God restored to Job all that was taken from him. Job even went on to live a good and a full life. And God wants to do the same for you.

***PRAYER REFLECTIONS
AND
NOTES***

It happened after this that the people of Moab with the people of Ammon, and others with them besides the Ammonites, came to battle against Jehoshaphat.
2 Chronicles 20:1

*O*ne of the hardest things for me to understand during the demise of my marriage was the timing. I was finally at a high point again in my walk with God. I was seeking His face and making changes for the better in my life. I felt I was a better wife and was really trying harder than I ever had before to make a great marriage. I was giving more than I thought possible. I was trying to be a true example of a godly woman. That is why it was difficult to understand the timing of attack on my marriage and the final outcome.

Sometimes we erroneously believe that when we are close to God and doing what is right, God will keep all evil away from us. We believe that attacks will not come because we are on the right path. But this just isn't true.

To believe such a lie serves only to deceive us when things go wrong. We begin to question our faith and even question God, Himself. The devil then uses this doubt against us in an effort to turn our hearts away from God and cause us to seek answers elsewhere.

Beloved, come to know that even if it were possible for you to walk in perfection, and it isn't, trials would still come. There'd still be mountains to climb.

Jehoshaphat revamped the whole country, city by city, mandating that all were to live by the commands of God. Jehoshaphat restored the people to God. It was after he had successfully done this, that the king of Moab, Ammon, and a host of other countries came up against Jehoshaphat.

Isn't it easy to understand enemy attack when you've done something wrong? But when you've been giving it your college best and living better than ever, it can really do a number on you when all hell breaks loose.

Don't become discouraged during such times. Don't turn away from God in the midst of an attack; turn toward Him. Don't allow satan to cause you to have disillusionment with your God. Instead, seek the face of God and watch Him work mightily on your behalf.

PRAYER REFLECTIONS AND NOTES

Yet I had planted you a noble vine, a seed of highest quality. How then have you turned before Me into the degenerate plant of an alien vine? Jeremiah 2:21

I recently spoke to a friend who is going through a divorce. She is having a very hard time understanding how easy it has been for her husband to dismiss their marriage vows. He not only has dismissed the vows, but he acts completely unconcerned about her or their children's welfare.

Her question seems to be "How can he completely forget almost two decades of our lives together? What has he done with all of the memories?" Her mind cannot conceive how he can appear so emotionally unattached.

I watch the hurt and the utter confusion wash over her mind as she attempts to figure it all out. But she nor I, nor any of us, will ever be able to make sense of anyone deciding to break up a family. Even God used terminology that alluded to how incomprehensible such behavior was.

In Jeremiah chapter 2, verse 21, God says, "Yet I had planted you a noble vine, a seed of highest quality. How then have you turned before Me into the degenerate plant of an alien vine?" God is basically saying, "What happened to you? How did you go from that to this?" Now I know I'm taking a little poetic license here, but they had traded God in for the pathetic idols that were all around them. They chose to leave God for that? Give me a break!

It was beyond comprehension how they could be disloyal to God after all that He had done for them. Perhaps, it's hard for you to understand how your spouse could turn away from all that you both built together. It might tear your heart in two to think of how quickly your spouse or ex-spouse has forgotten you.

But maybe you can find some comfort in knowing that God experienced the same thing with those He loved the most.

Take your heart to God because He understands what you are going through.

PRAYER REFLECTIONS AND NOTES

And in the thirty-ninth year of his reign, Asa became diseased in his feet, and his malady was severe; yet in his disease he did not seek the Lord, but the physicians.
2 Chronicles 16:12

There are so many situations that come into our lives that can grip us with fear and trembling. We might have always looked to God in the past, but find ourselves in a big mess this time. It reminds me of an old television show called Sandford and Son. Sandford often got into trouble, but when he felt there was no way out of a situation, he'd say to his deceased wife as he clutched his ailing heart, "This is the big one, Elizabeth. I'm coming to join you."

There are some things in life that really make you feel like you're down for the count. Divorce is one of those things. We might have turned to God for everything else, but divorce feels like the "big one." The temptation is to seek lawyers, friends, family advice, divorced co-workers, and just about anybody, but God. But God is "the One" with ALL the answers. And though I'm all for wise counsel, you'd best be seeking God first and foremost.

People can only give advice based on their experiences or someone else's. But God stands by His true and tested Word. In divorce or in any of our "diseases", let us not seek "the physicians" but the Lord.

God might send you to the "physicians" or He might lead you in another way. But whatever the case, get your marching orders from God.

And the satraps, administrators, governors, and the king's counselors gathered together, and they saw these men on whose bodies the fire had no power; the hair of their head was not singed nor were their garments affected, and the smell of fire was not on them.   Daniel 3:27

I remember sitting on the couch one night watching a young preacher on television. He stated that just as the three Hebrew boys went into the fiery furnace and came out with not even the scent of smoke on their clothes, we, too, could experience tragedy in our lives and be delivered from the pain of it.

As I sat there steeped in fresh pain, I found myself wondering if it could truly be so. It seemed like such an impossibility at the time. I really thought I would be forever scarred by the emotional and mental damage I had sustained. I thought I would not only have the scent of smoke on my life, but a charred heart to validate my actual encounter with the flames. I thought the painful memories of being led to the furnace, being shown the flames, and then being thrown in, would traumatize me forever.

It is so amazing to be able to say today that the fire had no power over me. The memory of it all does not haunt me. I can truly say I have forgiven all persons who were involved in that most painful of times in my life. I am convinced that my life would surely be a heap of ashes had it not been for Jesus Christ. I would probably have been somewhere searching for the latest self-help therapy to ease the pain. But the presence of Christ overcame any negative impact.

The Hebrew boys weren't the only ones who had Him as the fourth Person in the fiery furnace. He also walked with me through the fierce flames of divorce.

How shall I pardon you for this? Your children have forsaken Me. And sworn by those that are not gods. When I had fed them to the full, then they committed adultery and assembled themselves by troops in the harlots' houses. They were like well-fed lusty stallions; Every one neighed after his neighbor's wife.   Jeremiah 5:7-8

I often hear people who had a spouse walk out on them or mistreat them say, "I wonder what I did wrong or what I could have done better." It's as if we just naturally assume that if we are feeding someone and they are getting full, then they will stay put; contented, fat, and happy.

I see so many people turning cartwheels and jumping through hoops to "feed" their companion's hunger. They place a great deal of pressure on themselves to make sure the trough from which their spouse is eating from never goes empty. I have even heard people who were in a happy marriage, attribute it to their ability to keep the trough full, just short of implying that those of us who had gone through a divorce were just not adept at "trough filling." But my question to them is, "What if your spouse wandered out right after they finished eating from a full trough?"

In Jeremiah 5:7-8, God says of His people, "...when I had fed them to the full, THEN they committed adultery and assembled themselves by troops in the harlots' houses. They were like well-fed lusty stallions. Every one neighed after his neighbor's wife." Here we read how God gave them more than was sufficient. They are called "well-fed" not "barely satisfied," yet, God's generous provision still was not enough.

Do not allow others to place a guilt trip on you that somehow you just didn't do what it took to keep a person happy or a marriage together.

If people can be fed by the hand of God and still go looking elsewhere, don't beat yourself up too much over your trough-filling abilities.

PRAYER REFLECTIONS AND NOTES

And Amaziah did what was right in the sight of the Lord, but not with a loyal heart.
2 Chronicles 25:2

As I have gotten older and have pondered the ways of life and the world, I have often found the matter of living rather perplexing. I have realized that you can study things from an external perspective and still not know the heart of it all. For things can appear one way, but really be something altogether different. We look at people on the surface, yet God can see the hidden depths. That's why what is clearly visible to God can often completely escape us.

We can't comprehend the person who goes along appearing to be happily married and then all of a sudden leaves their spouse and children. They looked like the perfect person. They played the part so well.

Amaziah, too, looked the perfect part of king. He said and did all the right things. He appeared to be very godly, yet his heart was not loyal to God. Isn't that perplexing? "Amaziah did what was right in the sight of the Lord, but his heart was not right in the sight of the Lord."

This goes to show us that a person can have "all the say and all the do," but not have "any of the be," because being is a heart issue, while saying and doing are head issues. People can say "in love" things and do "in love" things but not "be" in love.

This knowledge really has helped me to understand some of the perplexities I have seen and still see in life. As a matter of fact, it helps me to process much of what I just couldn't understand about my own situation. I hope it has also helped you to process some of the perplexities in your life.

Now the word of the Lord came to Samuel saying, "I greatly regret that I have set up Saul as king for he has turned back from following Me and has not performed My commandments." And it grieved Samuel, and he cried out to the Lord all night.
1 Samuel 15:10-11

Regret. Deep, deep regret. If you are reading this book, you can certainly relate to regret. Oh, I am sure that there are many things for which you are grateful as a result of having married your spouse, especially if you have children. And there are also memories that were shared that you would never trade.

However, when you think of all that you've been through at the hand of the one you trusted, you feel deep regret. You can even regret that you ever met the person. Or you might regret that you chose him or her to be your marriage partner in the first place. You could be regretting the choices this person influenced you to make that now you have the sole responsibility for, such as decisions with financial implications, etc. Or what if you put off personal achievements for the sake of this person and now they are completely out of the picture.

Your life has been profoundly impacted by someone who has reneged on their contract; their covenant. And there is nothing you can do to make them honor it. You're left holding the bag and everything in the bag, whatever that might be.

Surely that can cause any human to feel a good deal of regret. But God? Could God ever understand regret? Could He possibly understand that human emotion? Of course, He could, and He does.

Saul was the man whom God had set up as leader of His people. Saul followed God for awhile and even accomplished much of what God had commanded him to do. But Saul later decided that he'd help God out and take matters into his own hands. He eventually forgot his covenant with God altogether and sought to do his own thing. It became all about Saul and none about God.

Saul was truly on the right path for awhile, but Saul changed. And when he changed, he made very poor decisions that affected the entire nation. God greatly regretted that He had made Saul leader.

You may have great regrets for the choice you made in your spouse, and unlike God, you didn't know the outcome. But do understand that your spouse may have started off right, but people can change for the worse. Don't deny the good that did come from it. Neither beat yourself over the head about the person you chose. You cannot control another person's actions.

Speak with God about the regrets you have. Even if no one else can relate, realize that God truly understands where you're coming from. He knows how it feels to have someone go back on the covenant. Yes, God understands regret.

PRAYER REFLECTIONS AND NOTES

Then Amaziah said to the man of God, "But what shall we do about the hundred talents which I have already given to the troops of Israel? And the man of God answered, The Lord is able to give you much more than this."   2 Chronicles 25:9

When I was at the end of my divorce, my ex-husband froze my bank account. Without a court order, but with "permission" from the judge, my account was completely emptied by he and his lawyer to pay for his staggering legal costs, and he was the one who filed for divorce. I felt so stripped and so violated. Not only was my bank account depleted, but my heart felt depleted, as well. I remember having a feeling of such waste. I had wasted an entire decade of my life, my energy, and my financial potential on someone who decided they didn't want to partner in this thing, after all.

About the time I was looking back with major regret, realizing that many of my youthful opportunities had been squandered on this failed relationship, I came upon this Scripture in the Bible.

Amaziah had the same questions you and I have. What do I do with all that I have given? It feels like such a waste. What will become of my investment? This was the way the man of God answered him: "The Lord is able to give you much more than this."

My heart leapt within me as I realized that this is my God, too. The same God that could give Amaziah much more than he had given, could do the same for me. I felt a peace and a hope at that moment that has been unshakable. Just the realization that what had been lost in the past doesn't really matter in God's economy, was very freeing to me. It's all about what God is going to give in this moment and in the future that makes all the difference.

I don't know what you've lost as a result of divorce. It could be financial resources, social status, a sense of identity, even loss of your children, or any number of things. But whatever you've lost, let me be like that man of

God who came to Amaziah. I can tell you from personal experience, the Lord is able to give you much, much more than what has been lost in the process.

PRAYER REFLECTIONS AND NOTES

God is our refuge and strength. A very present help in trouble.   Psalm 46:1

*T*here used to be a television program long ago called Beauty and the Beast. I can't remember exactly whom the actress was who played the beauty, nor the actor who played the beast, but I simply loved that show. It was a hit during my teen years and I could watch it a hundred times and still love the way the beast would come to "the beauty's" rescue.

She would try to handle a problem herself making sure that she had exhausted all resources, but then she would just call Vincent's name if she were in trouble. And Vincent would come running out of his cave and fiercely protect the woman he loved and the woman who was his friend.

Now, when you get right down to it, the show was a little hokey and definitely catered to a female audience. But for all intents and purposes, what woman doesn't want that kind of guy in her life? What man doesn't want to be viewed as some kind of knight in shining armor by the woman in his life?

Honestly, isn't that the way we kind of imagined it to be? We all want to be viewed favorably whether we are the beauty (the female) or the beast (the male). The woman wants to be the damsel in distress that is saved by the knight. The man wants to be the knight doing the saving.

How empty we feel when it doesn't turn out that way. How disillusioned we are when we realize that life doesn't work itself out in an hour, and really even less time if you count the commercial breaks in between. Perhaps, we, the television generation, really believe that all should work itself out with no loose ends to be tucked away. Perhaps, we decide it is not worth it when the guy is not quite the knight in shining armor and the lady is not quite the damsel in distress, but "de stressed damsel."

These dreams really become crushed when separation or divorce looms over a relationship. When one or the other walks out the door, so much for the Beauty and the Beast fairy tale. We can find ourselves waiting for it all to be a bad dream that we will just awaken from. But divorce is the reality and we no longer see the beauty and the ex winds up being the beast.

It is at this time that we can have difficulty trusting that anyone could ever be our "Vincent"; that one who comes to our rescue when we are in trouble. The one who can sense our pain and knows our needs.

But God not only can be this for us, but He is this for us. Our loving Father is just a whisper away. He wants us to call to Him in prayer when we find ourselves in trouble. He says to us that He is an ever-present help in the time of trouble. It doesn't matter how you got into trouble. That is not the point. The power is in the asking for help.

Vincent was just typecast by someone in Hollywood. But God is for real. You will see the power of this when you find yourself in trouble and then sincerely ask Him for help. God will be there in a hurry for you. Like no other you have ever known, He will be in your life what fairy tales are made of. If you are looking for someone who will never let you down, give God an opportunity in your life to show you what being there in trouble is all about. He loves you and wants to be the "Vincent" in your life. No one else can do this, unless, of course, it's scripted in Hollywood.

"What man of you, having a hundred sheep, if he loses one of them, does not leave the ninety-nine in the wilderness, and go after the one which is lost until he finds it? And when he has found it, he lays it on his shoulders, rejoicing." Luke 15:4-5

*T*here are those times in my life when I long to know that I am valuable beyond replacement to someone. I want to feel as if someone would fight against the world for my sake. I want to know that someone would search high and low if ever I were lost; that someone would endanger their very own life in order to save mine.

I know I sound like some sort of hopeless romantic, but the thought of someone leaving all else to come in pursuit of me really does something for me. Whenever I am discouraged and starting to feel a little down about who I am and my importance in life, all I have to do is think about the Bible story Jesus' told of the shepherd who lost the one sheep.

Now, I don't know much about shepherding, but 99 sheep are a lot of sheep. And I would figure that they all pretty much look alike, so how in the world would anyone really know the difference. But I have been told that shepherds know their sheep by name.

Another amazing thing to me is how any shepherd could leave the 99 in pursuit of the one lost sheep. That one sheep would have to be pretty valuable for the shepherd to leave the others in pursuit of it. Yet that is exactly the way Jesus describes how He feels about us. Do not ever think that you are not valuable or worth going after? Jesus, the good Shepherd, would leave everything, including His royal home in heaven, to come after you. Now, that should make you feel like royalty.

And whenever you are feeling lost and alone, just remember, you are "the one" that Jesus would leave all 99 for. He knows you by name and considers you of great worth.

O My Father, if it is possible, let this cup pass from Me; nevertheless, not as I will, but as You will." Matthew 26:39b

*H*ow I could so well relate to these words of Jesus in the garden. He wanted out of the situation and so did I. I wondered if there was any way around it. The present pain was so deep and the dread of what the future held horrified me. If the shadow of death was doing this to me, how would I bear the agony of the real thing: death of a marriage; death of a dream.

The anguish of the thought of no longer being the family we started out as, cut at the core of my being. What would I say? What would I do? How would I or could I raise three male children alone? I was placed in a situation I never ever thought I would be in. I had difficulties before, but nothing like this. I fought it for a while, but then decided what was going to be was going to be and I had to come to a place of acceptance.

My prayer became, "Let Your will be done in me and through me." I surrendered my will, my life, and my all to God. I no longer resisted the pain, but embraced it and allowed it to accomplish its perfect work in me. It wasn't easy then. Life isn't always easy now. But allowing God's will and not ours will always render the best results.

For God has delivered my soul from death. My eyes from tears and my feet from falling... Ps. 116:8

There are so many sweet things about newborn babies, but one of my favorites is watching them throw their tiny arms and hands up in the air while they're sleeping. Doctors call it startle reflex. It's as if they are dreaming of falling and so they reach out to whomever will catch them.

To help my sons feel more secure when they were infants, I would tightly wrap them in a blanket with their arms tucked inside to give them a greater sense of security.

The problems of life can make you feel a need for greater security. Divorce can definitely give you that "falling sensation." The only difference is, you're fully awake experiencing the fall. The events of our world can often go spiraling out of control leaving us reaching out for someone to catch us on the way down.

God is that Someone. His love for us is even greater than the love of a parent. He is the One Who formed us in our mother's womb. Therefore, He cares for us and desires for us to sense the love and security that only He can give.

Just as the newborn reaches out to be helped, we can reach out to our heavenly Father. He will tightly wrap His arms around us so that we will never have to fear the fall again. As today's Scripture states, "For God has delivered my soul from death, my eyes from tears, and my feet from falling..."

See I have engraved you on the palms of my hands; your walls are ever before me.
Isaiah 49:16

I remember working with a guy who had a tattoo on his arm of his wife's name written through a heart. He was a bodybuilder and always wore muscle shirts, so you could always see his wife's name on his bulging biceps. I am by no means advocating tattoos, but I just remember greatly admiring that particular tattoo.

That tattoo said to the world that this man loved this woman and that the permanency of that tattoo was a small reflection of the permanency of his love for her. No other woman could ever see him and not know that this woman was number one in his life. She would be forever etched in his heart, even as her name was engraved on his arm.

I often desired my former spouse to do something so crazily romantic for me. Something that said he would always treasure and cherish me.

Something that said he would put me above all others forever and ever, amen.

After the divorce, I found myself wondering to whom I was really significant. To whom did I matter? Did the pain I was feeling grieve the heart of anyone else?

God answered those questions for me in Isaiah 49:16, when He said, "See, I have engraved you on the palms of my hands; your walls are ever before me." Ain't that something? If that don't beat all. God, Himself, has a tattoo of me.

I don't have to search any further for someone who would do something so crazily romantic for me. God loves me so much and He loves you so much, that He has engraved our names on His palm.

Even a bicep is covered sometimes, especially in the winter. But a palm is always seen by everyone, including the person tattooed. It is a constant reminder to everyone of a deep and passionate love. To read this in the Bible makes me feel incredibly special to God. He's so crazy about us that He wants to see our names constantly. That thrills me to the core. His love for us is permanent. He won't divorce us in pursuit of another.

Every time God raises His hand, looks at His hand, waves His hand, or places His hand upon the arm of His throne, our names will always be right there, ever before Him.

PRAYER REFLECTIONS AND NOTES

But Jesus looked at them and said, "With man it is impossible, but not with God; for with God all things are possible."
Mark 10:27

I had so many dreams of what old age would hold for me and the one I had chosen as a husband. We would have children together whom we would love and raise the best way we knew how. We would pray for them, nurture them, and navigate them through the perils of life. We would laugh with them and cry with them and celebrate this most precious gift of our union.

Ahh, the joy that would fill our hearts as we watched our boys grow into men. I often had thoughts of us sitting beside one another talking about what the children had done when they were younger. I always thought we would question one another on where the time had gone and how could they be all grown up now. I could see us clasping one another's hands and silently knowing that somehow, by

God's grace, we had made this most miraculous of journeys together. We had shared this wondrous passage of time. Without a word, we would console one another's hearts as we missed our children. Without a word, our eyes would say to each other that we were glad for all the time that we did have together as a family.

And yet, that scenario would never be. That future hope was obliterated by the dissolution of the marriage. It seems so strange that when the death of a marriage takes place, the death of so many dreams takes place, as well. You not only have to find new things to fill your life, but you must also find new dreams to fill your heart.

But know that God will take your hurt, your heart, and your broken dreams. He loves you so much and wants you to pour it all out before Him. He wants to hear from you what it is you are feeling. He wants you to tell Him about all the dreams from that phase of your life that will never be. He, in turn, will lovingly show you all the possibilities right now and for the future. He will let you know that life is by no means over for you. He will provide you with a safe place to come and be real about all that ever was and all that you had hoped it would ever be.

My Father is the One who can restore you. He is the One who can place you back on your feet again. He is the One who can fill your heart with dreams again; great big dreams. Dreams that require your dependency upon Him. Wonderful and hopeful dreams. Dreams that can come true for you because it is God's good pleasure to grant them to you.

There is something special in just knowing that the God of this universe desires for you and me to obtain our dreams. With that knowledge alone, know that you can begin again and you can dream again.

PRAYER REFLECTIONS AND NOTES

Now, O Lord God, let Your promise to David my father be established, for You have made me king over a people like the dust of the earth in multitude. Now give me wisdom and knowledge, that I may go out and come in before this people; for who can judge this great people of Yours?"
2 Chronicles 1:9-10

*P*arenting is rewarding, but equally challenging. I care so much about whether or not my children serve God with a whole heart. I try to train them up in the way that they should go, but I often feel like instead of simply knowing the way that they should go, I have to keep stopping and pulling out the map. I do read God's Word and I follow the instructions as best as I can. But there's something to be said for having had healthy patterns to follow.

I try very hard, but as a single parent, I have sometimes felt exhausted as I tried to figure out the right way to handle a given situation.

It seems Solomon had that "Johnny on the spot" kind of wisdom that gave him instantaneous knowledge of how to handle any dilemma. The Word says he asked God for that very wisdom to help him discern how to lead those in his kingdom.

Our homes are our very own kingdom. Our children are those that God has given to us to lead and to train up. Solomon felt incapable of handling such a great task on his own. He didn't want to operate by "trial and error" just winging it. He didn't want to mess up people's lives. He really wanted insight into the black and white of godly leadership. So he asked God to give him wisdom.

So I stop right now. I take a deep breath in and I exhale. With my eyes closed and my heart bowed, I pray. I ask You, God of the heavens and the earth, the future, past, and present; please give me wisdom in all areas, but right now I'm focusing in on parenting. I need Your supernatural discernment in the many situations that arise with my children. I want to be a good leader for my children. Please bless those who are reading this book to have that wise leadership, too. Guide us and give us peace as we parent. In Jesus name, I pray. Amen.

PRAYER REFLECTIONS AND NOTES

You can rely upon God's love. 1 John 4:13

Good help is so hard to find. It seems that people are very unreliable in so many ways and the products that are made by them are often equally unreliable.

How many times do we bring something home that promises to do something for us? Then we get that item all geared up for performance only to watch it fall apart or not quite do what it claims it can. We feel so frustrated and angry that we ever believed the advertisement and bought the product in the first place. Now we have to turn around and take that product back to where we got it from in order to get our money back. What a major inconvenience! But somehow we feel a little better in knowing that at least we can get a refund on our hard-earned cash.

Many products even sucker you into buying them just because they have the money-back guarantee. They promise us that they will deliver a certain benefit and we have nothing to lose by trying it. They will even pay our postage to return it. It makes it so much easier to take that leap when you know that you are losing nothing.

But what about marriage, in which there are no guarantees? You cannot turn around and take it back with no risks attached. Once you have made that marital commitment, intertwined your lives, and often even added children to the mix, there are lifetime affects if "the product" doesn't deliver. The inconveniences are not minor, but life-changing, when a marriage doesn't deliver what it promised it would. The pain of this product failure has more far-reaching consequences than any other earthly relationship. When we find that this relationship has come up short and is unreliable, it is easy to lose faith in all things.

However, our Lord Jesus Christ is very reliable. We can place all of our stock in Him and not worry about whether or not we can depend on Him.

We never have to worry about Him letting us down like all the others did. He is faithful and true. No matter where we go, who we are, or what we've done, we can readily rely on God's love for us. His love will never fail us. His love will always stand up to any test and prove to rank the highest of all other structures that we could rely on. God's love is the only thing that we can know is fully guaranteed.

Allow yourself to receive all the love, the joy, the peace, and every good gift that He wants to lavish upon you. Simply open your heart and hands to receive a completely guaranteed gift. Don't be afraid at all. He would never try to pull a fast one on you. God will do what He says He will do and God is Who He says He is. Life-back guarantee.

PRAYER REFLECTIONS AND NOTES

So I said, "Oh, that I had wings like a dove! I would fly away and be at rest. Indeed, I would wander far off, and remain in the wilderness. I would hasten my escape from the windy storm and tempest. Psalm 55:6-8

*T*here are those days when I am so utterly exhausted and mentally maxed out that I really would like for Calgon to take me away. Of course, I have all kinds of ideas for mental escapades that would be nice. It is not that I don't love what I do, because I love my children and I love my life. Most of the time, I am really on top of my game and feeling pretty great. But there are those dark days when it seems like a cloud descends over my mind and every molehill is a mountain and every mistake on my part is utter ruin for life. I am not sure why I sink into this place from time to time, but I believe that sometimes life is just hard. And what exactly constitutes hard is different for everyone. My hard may not be your hard and your hard may not be mine.

But there are things that just get to us that cause us to feel like we wish we could fly away from it all.

David felt this way. He said, "Oh, if I could just have wings so that I could fly away." I can really relate to "the shepherd boy turned king". There were times during the divorce process that I just wanted to escape from it all. And there are still times in life when I feel like I would like a hammock, some lemonade, and a call to let me know when the parade starts up. But that is just a wee bit unrealistic. We cannot join the hammock for life club and swing our lives into a new paradigm.

What we can do is realize that God does allow us to escape to Him in prayer. We can carry all of our needs to Him at any place or at any time. God will always be there willing to take us up into His wings of love.

We have the privilege to go before Him with everything within our hearts and lay it before our God.

Instead of letting Calgon take you away, just let Jesus take you away in His love.

Therefore He is also able to save to the uttermost those who come to God through Him, since He always lives to make intercession for them. Hebrews 7:25

*H*ave you ever heard the expression "I live for Friday?" I've also heard people say that they live for the weekend, or for football, or for shopping, or for Christmas, and the list goes on and on.

Jesus also had His own phrase for what He lived for. His phrase was even more emphatic than any of these others. He said, "...He always lives to make intercession for us." Isn't that awesome? Jesus lives for "praying for you and me." That's what He lives for. He's always standing in our corner like Mickey stood for Rocky. He's the One yelling at us from the sidelines as we're lying flat on the ground. He's saying, "Get up! You can do it." He's asking God to help us. He's watching each tear that falls from our eyes. He sees each weight upon our hearts. He's taking it

ALL into account. He believes in us and cheers for us no matter how bad things may appear.

The rest of this Scripture reads, "He is also able to save to the uttermost those who come to God through Him." No matter how lost your cause may seem, Jesus can save you completely. Don't feel as if you're all alone and that no one even cares what happens to you. Even though people might stop caring, God will always care. People grow weary of praying for you when they don't see results soon enough. But I can guarantee you of One Who just can't get you off His mind.

Some may live for the weekend. Some may live for a cause. But Jesus lives to stand in your corner and to see you through every thing that will come your way in this life. Just knowing that, ought to give you "something to live for."

They confronted me in the day of my calamity; But the Lord was my support.
2 Samuel 22:19

Sonya, do you have any support? Hmm, let's ponder that question. Just exactly what kind of support should I be expecting from anyone? What do people really mean when they ask me if I have support? Support. There are all kinds of support out there.

There are support hose for the woman who wants to give her legs that perfectly shaped look. There are support panties that give you that little extra tug in the tummy. They give the appearance that the five children you have all around you never left any permanent alterations to your girlish figure. There are support braces for knees and elbows to give them the necessary strength they need to perform the tasks they have always done. There is shoe support that gives you the extra cushioning to go the distance with less fatigue. There are support bras that give women an added lift when either size or gravity or both has made it most welcoming to receive a little reinforcement. Many ex-spouses have to pay support. Support, support, what exactly do others mean when they ask if I have support?

I once heard a very popular radio talk show host say that she was once asked if she would rather have her husband die or to have him divorce her. She said that she would rather have him die because at least people would bring her food. Don't you just love that response. And for anyone who has ever gone through a divorce, that little response is often painfully true.

People will do and say many things during a divorce, but they very seldom know how to reach out to you and offer you support. I know I am being somewhat comical with my approach to this "support issue," but I do understand what people are trying to ask me.

Friends and family mean well, but they don't really know how to give you the support that you often need. Others don't give the support because they are too busy trying to judge you for being separated or divorced in the first place.

I found that the best thing for me to do was to take my needs to God and to let Him be my Source of strength. He is my support! I have found it so much easier to just get on my knees and lay out all my problems before God. I try not to place such a burden on others anymore. They don't even know how they are going to come through their own situations, much less navigate me through mine.

So I don't *expect* support from others. I am just thoroughly grateful for whatever I get whenever I get it. But God is He Who holds the whole world in its place. And since He does such an awesome job at that, we can rely on Him to support us through whatever places we find ourselves in.

Hmm, do I have support? You betcha! I've got the support of God's everlasting arms sustaining me and you can have that too.

***PRAYER REFLECTIONS
AND
NOTES***

Then they cried out to the Lord in their trouble, and He brought them out of their distresses. He caused the storm to be still, so that the waves of the sea were hushed. Then they were glad because they were quiet; So He guided them to their desired haven.   Psalm 107:28-29 (NASB)

How often I have heard of the drowning person who is struggling desperately not to die. A person comes to help him and the drowning person kicks, flails, and climbs on the very person who is trying to save him. It almost causes that person to drown too. There have been instances where both people have actually drowned.

I thought of this being similar to drowning in the sea of divorce. I remember feeling as if I were drowning. I wanted someone, anyone, to take away the pain I felt flooding over my soul. I felt so helpless over my condition.

That must be what a drowning person feels. Here they are, with all of this water surrounding them. They find themselves in a situation where they are unable to save themselves from what they are completely immersed in. They slap at water, they fight, and they use all of their energies to not be swallowed up. They find all of their effort to be futile. Their only help is a source outside of themselves.

In divorce, we often look for that source in other people. We hope they can somehow save us. But what we often do is kick, flail, and climb on them until we drown them in our sorrow. They are now unable to help us to the great extent that we need help. There is only one Source that can save us.

There is only One Who can draw us from the waters that would otherwise overcome us. His name is Jesus. He is the One who can be there past midnight when your friends have gone to sleep. He's the only One who can hold you during the wee hours of the morning when all you can do is cry. It is Jesus who can swim out to you and save you from a desperate situation.

Call out to Him. Cry for His help. Open your heart to His sweet, sweet Word and allow it to lift you to a place of safety.

PRAYER REFLECTIONS AND NOTES

Let us therefore come boldly to the throne of grace; that we may obtain mercy and find grace to help in time of need. Hebrews 4:16

Yesterday I was coming home from a church event and the traffic was really backed up for that time of night. Normally that particular highway was not crowded and it was rather easy to get to where I was going.

However, this night was quite an exception. All three lanes were bumper to bumper. I put my signal on to ask the persons in the other lane if I may get over. I just watched car after car squeeze as closely as they could to keep me out. And my thought was, with traffic moving this slowly, does it really matter if one more car gets in front of you? Is it really going to put you at your destination any sooner to hog every inch of space on the highway? What do you have to lose by letting me in?

Because no one was going to let me in, I had to revert to my Miami style of driving. That means you make a path for your car where one does not exist. Thank God, I maneuvered my way in and got to where I was going without having to miss my exit.

I could not help but thinking of how many times I had felt that way as a divorcee in the church. I would show up to an event as a divorced single mom with my three small children and I was often met with unspoken judgment or silent disapproval. I so desired to be valued based on the content of my character or my worth in the eyes of God and not on my circumstances.

It can sometimes seem like a divorced Christian who remains single is often looked upon to give explanation for his or her "failure." And in my case, where many people assumed that I was married, they felt a need to know what happened in a case like mine where I appeared to be so "normal" and so happy.

I praise God that whenever I put my signal on with Him because I need to "get over," He is more than willing to "let me in." He is more interested in me not passing "the exit" than I am. It just doesn't matter to God where we have been, if our hearts before Him are right. Who can make a determination about our hearts except God?

Come into the presence of your God through the blood of Jesus Christ and enter into His love and acceptance of you. Talk to Him about whatever is on your heart. Go ahead and put your signal on and watch the Father "let you in."

***PRAYER REFLECTIONS
AND
NOTES***

And my God shall supply all your need according to His riches in glory by Christ Jesus. Philippians 4:19

Tonight at my Wednesday night Bible study, we were discussing how it is God's desire for us to be completely satisfied with Him. We so often find ourselves looking to other people or other things to satisfy us. We talked about if people are upset or angry, they tend to try to appease themselves with all kinds of things. Some try food, some try shopping, some try alcohol, some try drugs, some escape through television, some escape through relationship after relationship to try to fill their emptiness.

An incredible void can seem to overtake you when you have experienced a divorce or separation. When you are used to someone being "there" for you and with you, then all of a sudden their presence is physically and emotionally gone, you can really be left feeling alone and empty. It is such a normal response to want to hurry up and replace that empty feeling with something else or someone else right away. It would seem that the replacement sure would beat the feeling of emptiness and pain.

However, where matters of the heart are concerned, we must go back to the manufacturer. God is the One who created our hearts. He knows what to do to fix us. He knows exactly how to satisfy the longing we feel within. Nothing else or no one else will do. That is a fact. Something or someone might give a sensation of fullness for awhile, but the temporary effect of such a replacement will only leave us in greater want.

Here is an analogy that might help. I am a single mom with three young children. When it comes to shopping, which I am not crazy about anyway, I like to go to one place. Whenever I have had to make about three different stops or more to get various items, I am so flustered and outdone, that I am irritable and tired by the time I am finished. However, when I go to a "super-center" where I can get groceries, clothes, shoes, school supplies, and pharmaceuticals, I am in hog heaven. I don't have to lug children from store to store or write another check, because I can get all of my needs met right there in one place.

That's how it is with God. We can have all of our needs met by Him. He is the One person that we can go to and be assured that we will have to search no further. I don't have to worry about coming to God and then needing something from another place because He ran out of what I needed or He didn't quite satisfy all of my desires. No, quite the opposite is true. God exceeds my expectations *when* I go to Him to meet my needs.

I know that my God and Father will do the same for you. Go to Him and allow His peace to flood your soul. Try Him and see that He is the best one stop shop there is.

***PRAYER REFLECTIONS
AND
NOTES***

I returned and saw under the sun that the race is not to the swift; nor the battle to the strong; nor bread to the wise; nor riches to men of understanding; nor favor to men of skill; but time and chance happen to them all.   Ecclesiastes 9:11

Today, while listening to the radio, I heard a woman speaking about marriage and her relationship with their husband. She was an excellent speaker, but she said something that pricked me a little when I heard it. I turned the radio on about the time I heard her say that she would like to meet the woman that would try to take her husband. She said that she does everything she can to see to it that her husband is taken care of.

I knew exactly where she was coming from and took no offense in the heart of the message. However, listening from the vantage point of a divorced woman, the statement rang with a hint of arrogance on her part. I do not know whether or not this woman was being arrogant, but it was probably more of a lack of understanding that often occurs on the part of many women and men who have not been divorced.

It's funny how it is so easy to accept a good portion of the credit for the success of a marriage when it is still together. But after having analyzed the divorced and the still-married, I have come to see that the only difference between the two lies in the grace of God.

Many people that I know who are still married happen to be products of the "time and chance" principle that Solomon so appropriately addressed. Perhaps, opportunities or obstacles that presented themselves to one family did not present themselves to the other. This does not discredit those spouses who have done a great job trying to care for one another's needs. But we have to realize that a person who decides to give up on a relationship and/or pursue another has to make that choice within himself.

Marriage is a collective "union" made up of individual choices. I tend to liken it to a see-saw. It takes two to make it work, but at any given time, the other person can hop off. Does this mean that a person's choice to remain on the see-saw depends on the see-sawing on the other side or is it simply a matter of decision?

I've come to believe that on the playground of marriage, much has to do with each individual choosing daily that he or she is on the see-saw for life, no matter what other equipment is on the playground, nor who else comes to play. This is a choice made from within.

A marriage working is a mystery we should stand in awe of and thankfulness to God for. We should take little credit for it, realizing that but by the grace of God, we, too, could be on the see-saw alone.

PRAYER REFLECTIONS AND NOTES

And when they saw Him walking on the sea, they supposed it was a ghost and cried out; for they all saw Him and were troubled. But immediately He talked with them and said to them, "Be of good cheer! It is I; do not be afraid."   Mark 6:49

My standard term to express out of control moments is "wigging out." I'm not sure where this term came from, but it would be my perfect choice of words to describe what the disciples must have felt when they were peacefully sailing in their boat when all of a sudden a storm broke out. The waves caused from this storm were so high they overlapped the boat. These strong, burly men were terrified.

To make matters worse, they see what appears to be a ghost walking on the water and coming straight toward them. By this time, it would have been over for me. I would have gone from "wigging out" to "wigged out." Here these poor guys were, on this boat alone in the middle of the sea, and this ferocious storm comes out of nowhere.

Now, Jesus knew this was going to happen. He knew they would be out there alone and afraid to the point of death. Why didn't He just let them know that the storm was on the way and not to worry about it because He would come and bring peace and calm to the situation? Is it because this would have required no faith?

I believe it was His plan for them to experience huge waves, to feel the rocking and the reeling of the boat, and to feel water violently splashing in their eyes to the point of blinding their sight; and yet, still be convinced within their hearts that He would take care of them. He wanted their trust and their confidence. He wanted them to have unshakable faith.

Jesus knows your present situation and your future too. There is no storm in your life that is a surprise to Jesus. He knows in advance what will happen.

So don't wig out. Keep your hair on. Trust and have faith in Jesus that just as He came through in your past, He will come through for you in the present. Just place your hand in the hand of the Man who stills the water and calms the sea.

PRAYER REFLECTIONS AND NOTES

He sent His word and healed them, And delivered them from their destructions.
Psalm 107:20

*Y*esterday I went to a home-going service or what many would call a funeral. I watched as my friend was met with love and support through hugs and kisses from family, friends, and even people she had never met before. Her husband had passed at the age of 47. Somehow that caused even greater compassion. Some shared words of encouragement. Others simply shared themselves and allowed their presence to convey the message. No matter how we came, we were all saying the same thing: "We love you and we grieve this loss with you." We were all so sad this had happened to her and her 8 year-old daughter.

This loss made no sense to us despite the fact that we accepted God's sovereignty. We all reached out to her and took a piece of her pain in an effort to lighten her load. It was as if I could see her being carried by our love.

How similar the deep feelings of loss are in death and divorce. But with death, one can at least come to terms with the sovereignty of God. All must die at some point and God chooses when that point will be. No one has much say in the matter.

However, a divorce is quite different. You still feel the same deep pain. You still feel an intolerable sense of emptiness. You still have that nagging hurt in the pit of your stomach that seems to never go away. You ache with a longing for what was and yet will never be again. But in the case of divorce, there is little explanation. Especially when you're the one who didn't initiate it. You've got all the death feelings, sandwiched between rejection. No ceremony takes place to help you say your final goodbye because there really isn't one. There is no real sense of closure.

There are few hugs, fewer kisses, and much judgment. No one brings food, no cards are sent, and friends feel awkward about the whole thing. You not only lose your life partner, but many times you lose all the family relationships that came with the other person. There is loss upon loss. There is insult upon injury. There is a deeply intense emotional pain that must be worked through with the help and power of God or your wounds will never heal.

But that doesn't have to be. Through the Word of God, which is flowing with life, you can be replenished and revived. There is life in the Word that can resurrect the deadness of your soul.

Administer the Word to your wounded heart, as you would administer medicine to a sick body. As you have faith in a pharmaceutical prescription to heal your body, place even greater faith in the spiritual prescription of the Word of God. Make it a daily discipline and just watch its power to heal, take effect in your life this day.

PRAYER REFLECTIONS AND NOTES

When they had come to the land of Zuph, Saul said to his servant who was with him, "Come, let us return, lest my father cease caring about the donkeys and become worried about us." And the servant said to him, "Look now, there is in this city a man of God, and he is an honorable man; all that he says surely comes to pass. So let us go there; perhaps he can show us the way that we should go."   *I Samuel 9:5-6*

For many people who are now divorced, their spouses were their best friend. If that was the case for you, you probably feel like you not only lost a marriage partner who helped in the day- to- day routines of life, but you also lost your confidante.

It is very important for you to fill this void of friendship and companionship in your life with godly people who will be of help to you, and preferably of the same gender. These are people who can help you through the tough times. These are the people who help you find a way out of no way. They spur you to go on until you reach your potential. They won't take no from you. They push you onward when you've lost your way.

This was the kind of person that Saul's servant was to him. Saul had lost his donkeys and didn't know how to find them. He wanted to throw the towel in and go back home. His attitude was "let the donkeys be lost, but it's time to go home." His servant encouraged him to continue on. His servant told him to go and get the help he needed from a reliable source, the prophet. Saul was still seeing the negative side because he said that he had nothing to offer this prophet who might help him. His servant rose to the occasion, yet again, and said that he would give to the prophet from his own resources all the silver that he had. The servant finally convinced Saul to try.

Once Saul got to the prophet, not only were his donkeys found, his destiny was discovered. This prophet was the very one who anointed him to be king. Without a loyal servant and friend, Saul would have turned around discouraged, defeated, and donkeyless. Instead, he met with destiny and the donkeys were found to boot.

Surround yourself with people who encourage you onward and who won't allow you to leave your donkeys lost or your destiny undiscovered.

PRAYER REFLECTIONS AND NOTES

Truly my soul silently waits for God; From Him comes my salvation. He only is my rock and my salvation; He is my defense; I shall not be greatly moved.
Psalm 62:1-2

Yes, truly my soul does wait silently for God. From Him alone comes my salvation.

It seems more and more that I am learning the truth of this simple, yet potent Bible verse. I am not sure if it is because I am maturing as a person, or life becomes more difficult as you get older, or a combination of the two. But whatever the reason, I am seeing that I can always expect salvation from God. I cannot put my dependence on any person to bring rest to my soul and salvation to my situation. It is God alone Who can do that. I might as well not even try to seek fulfillment or answers outside of God.

The true and lasting peace I have received have come from God and through God. Whenever I have turned to any outside source for strength or answers, I have always come up short. I might add, however, that if outside sources pointed me to Jesus, I did find strength there, as well. But once again, the strength came from the Source. When we come to realize that God truly is our Source and He does desire to save us in every situation in life, it is then that we can wait silently for Him. We can know with full assurance that He will show up.

This reminds me of my eldest son when he was just a little guy. I had him in preschool two days a week. Every time I would come and pick him up, I could see him silently waiting for me to come and get him. He knew I was coming and he always ran to greet me with a big smile and huge hug. He could wait silently because he trusted I was coming. He didn't have to scream and yell and throw a tantrum at a certain hour. Even if I was running a little late and he was the only one there, I always found him silently waiting. He was assured of my love. He knew I wanted to come and get him, as much as he wanted to be gotten. It was a clear understanding.

I also want you to clearly understand that God can be trusted. He loves you like no one else ever has or ever will. You can wait silently for Him. He'll be sure to come and get you.

PRAYER REFLECTIONS AND NOTES

*From the nations of whom the Lord had said to the children of Israel, "You shall not intermarry with them, nor they with you. Surely they will turn away your hearts after their gods." Solomon clung to these in love.
I Kings 11:2*

Clung. The word, clung. I don't recall the word clung being used in any other passage of the Bible like it is used in this one. I'm not saying that the word clung is nowhere else in the Bible, but it really hit me when I read it concerning the life of Solomon.

It is such a needy word. It is a word of deep and vulnerable desire. It's an expression denoting a shameless clutching onto a person or a thing. I envision a pitiful persona grabbing onto the ankles of someone who is trying to walk away.

Clung. Solomon; the wisest, most powerful, wealthiest, king who ever lived, with the grandest kingdom there ever was, CLUNG. Solomon, clung. He clung to these in love. He clung to what he should have never even allowed his fingertips to touch in the first place.

Sometimes we are like Solomon and we cling. We cling to people who are walking away. We cling to memories that are long in our past. We clutch onto the ankles of yesterday for fear of walking into tomorrow without this thing that we are clinging to. But when we cling to anything other than God, then that thing becomes our idol. And idols turn our hearts away from God. And once we allow anything or anyone to turn our hearts away from God, we can no longer be loyal in our love to Him or for Him.

Release yesterday. Stop clinging to your past or something or someone in your past. Just as an acrobat on the flying trapeze let's go of the bar to grab ahold of the hand of another acrobat; let go of what was and grab ahold of the hand of God.

Unlike Solomon, let's write a different ending to our story. How does "and they clung to God in love" sound? Yes, that sounds much, much better.

Then he went down and talked with the woman; and she pleased Samson well. After some time, when he returned to get her, (he turned aside to see the carcass of the lion. And behold, a swarm of bees and honey were in the carcass of the lion.
Judges 14:7-8

Why do people hold onto things that they know are a detriment to them? Why do people get into ruts and then knowingly choose to stay in them? I can gain some wisdom from my own life in answering this question, but we can also gain wisdom from Samson's life. Samson made some pretty poor choices, especially when it came to companionship. He chose to remain in a dead-end relationship with Delilah even though he knew she didn't have his best interests at heart. He was holding onto something "dead" to satisfy an inner hunger that he had. There was a lust and desire within that kept leading him back to Delilah.

The same thing happened with him when he saw the dead carcass of the lion. He reached inside of it to satisfy a longing for something sweet. He was a Nazirite who had vowed to stay away from dead things, yet here he was touching what he had no business touching. It wasn't as if he didn't know whether the lion was dead or not. There was a hollow body of dry bones lying on the street with a beehive in it. That pretty much constitutes dead.

Delilah was no different. She also possessed what appeared to be sweetness within, however, Delilah was a dead thing along Samson's path. He knew Delilah was a hollow body of dry bones like the carcass of the lion, yet he stayed in the relationship anyway.

Delilah was not Samson's wife. There was no marital commitment that kept him there. So why the attachment?

When analyzing myself and others who at one time or another chose "dead things," I realized that most of the time we actually knew they were dead. Our own emptiness and hunger led us to them and caused us to stay.

If you find yourself in a "dead" situation or a dead-end relationship because divorce or something else has left you feeling empty and unloved, get out now. If you are fooling around in fornication, adultery, or anything that you know is a "dead thing," stop.

I can understand your emptiness. I have felt emptiness, too. But let God fill the void in your heart. Nothing else or no one else will do. Don't touch what is unholy and go against the commands of God to meet your needs. To continue in sin will cause you to lose your vision, but will ultimately cost you your life. Take it from Samson. He learned that lesson the hard way.

PRAYER REFLECTIONS AND NOTES

I *charge you, O daughters of Jerusalem; Do not stir or awaken love until it pleases.*
Song of Solomon 8:4

After I had been single again for some time, I began experiencing something very strange and difficult for me to understand. I was feeling such a longing to be wanted and to be needed by someone. I was desiring to share my wealth of love and affection with someone whom I had chosen as my own.

It is only natural to want to love someone in a close and intimate fashion and to have that intimacy reciprocated. I wondered if that was the place where I had reached the next level. The mature level of feeling strongly but having to put those feelings aside until a later time; a proper time. I knew that the proper time for these feelings to be shared with another had not come yet. They were stored away within me the same way Christmas gifts are stored until Christmas day. Yes, they are there, but only to be opened at the appointed time. To open them earlier would be to ruin the joy and delight of Christmas. To open them early would be to eliminate the element of surprise. And one of the most precious joys of Christmas is that element of surprise.

The surprise and joy would be taken from us if we prematurely opened these hidden gifts within. We cannot allow ourselves to tear open these valuable packages. We must wait on God to bring about the right time for us to share that which is so wonderfully precious with the one of His choosing, within the confines of marriage. To do anything other than that would prove to be a deep regret.

And you are complete in Him, Who is the head of all principality and power. Colossians 2:10

*I*t is such a temptation for many who are divorced to hurry into another relationship. The need to feel loved and to be desired by someone can at times be overwhelming. We are made in the image of God and God is a Giver, the greatest Giver of all. We find ourselves wanting to give the love away.

However, it is not a good idea to quickly enter into another relationship. Marriage is a union that bonds two people to become one flesh. A divorce is an actual ripping and tearing apart of this flesh. If you rush into another relationship quickly, you are not giving yourself proper time to heal. Your heart is still vulnerable and in a very delicate condition. Your emotions are still in need of strengthening.

There is a great need for you to reflect over the dynamics of the failed marriage. What can you extract from it that can make you better and make you stronger?

The more time you give yourself to heal, the stronger you will become. You can better determine who you really are and what you really want from a relationship. If you're not careful, you can fulfill your temporary desires with a permanent disaster. That's worth saying again. Don't meet a temporary desire with a permanent decision. I have told myself this over and over and it has helped me to keep things in perspective.

Giving myself plenty of time to heal has been incredibly beneficial to me. I have not only learned to enjoy myself more, but I have really learned how to enjoy God more and to have my needs met by Him. The awesome thing about having your needs met by God is that He ALWAYS satisfies. I never ever come away from God feeling used or empty. I come away feeling filled, valued, empowered, and tremendously special. I know that allowing God to build me up has caused me to be incredibly grounded and judicious in who and what I will allow into my life.

This in itself has precipitated an attraction from others who admire the wholeness they see in me.

But right now, I'm really learning to love the God Who made me. And I'm learning to love the me God made. I encourage you to do the same. Go with God and let Him heal your heart and complete you in His presence. Then you can discover what it is you really want from yourself, from others, and from the life that you live.

PRAYER REFLECTIONS AND NOTES

Nevertheless the people refused to listen to the voice of Samuel; and they said, "No, but we will have a king over us, that we also may be like all the nations, and that our king may judge us and go out before us and fight our battles." 1 Samuel 8:19-20

*I*t has been said that the world was designed for couples. Everything seems to cater more to a couple and not to a single person. Oftentimes when you go to restaurants, plays, movies, or whatever it is that you are accustomed to do for entertainment, you are surrounded by couples.

When you are first separated or divorced, this can be a bit intimidating. It is very awkward to come on the scene as a single person when you're used to making your appearance with someone by your side. Inwardly, you might be at a place where you are getting used to being alone and trusting God to complete you, but when inundated with couples all around, you might be tempted to just have someone there because everyone else does. Everyone else seems to have someone to go to functions and events with. Everyone else has two parents for their children. What everyone else has can sometimes contemptuously yell at you from the sidelines of life. You can begin to feel the gnaw "to be like everyone else" no matter what the consequences are.

That is what the Israelites wanted. Samuel tried to tell them what having a king would really be like. Samuel basically told them that it would make their lives much more difficult and much more complicated than it was at the moment. He tried to warn them of the strain this arrangement would place upon their lives. Samuel was trying to get them to see that they had a lot more freedom than the neighboring countries that had kings.

The Israelites' focus was on none of these facts, but only on what the other people had. They had God, Himself, as their Leader. Yet, the Bible tells us that this was their response to Samuel; "Nevertheless, the people refused to obey the voice of Samuel; and they said,

'No, but we *WILL* have a king over us that we may also be like all the other nations'..."

Isn't that sad? The Israelites didn't know how to appreciate their present condition. They had it made in the shade and traded it all to be just like everyone else.

My friend, I'm not saying you are to never get remarried. I'm just saying decide to immensely enjoy where you are at until God chooses a "king" for you, if ever He desires for you to have one. Trust Him. He knows what's best for you. And what's best is what He wants you to have!

PRAYER REFLECTIONS AND NOTES

These all wait for You, that You may give them their food in due season. What you give them they gather in; You open Your hand, they are filled with good.
Psalm 104: 27-28

Every family has its vices. One of ours is doughnuts. Yes, there are many other vices, but this is the one I'll let you in on.

The boys and I went to the store to pick up a few things. They twisted my arm into buying a box of doughnut holes. To complement this treat, I also bought a fresh gallon of milk. Could anything be more perfect?

We got home and eagerly tore into those doughnuts holes, only to realize that they weren't even fresh. They were dry and stale.

I told the boys not to touch them because I was taking them back to get a fresh batch. When I finally got ready to take the doughnuts back to the store, the container was half-empty. I was very disappointed with my sons because first of all, they had disobeyed me. Secondly, I would not very well be able to justify returning stale doughnuts that were half-eaten. I could see the customer service person saying, "Did it take ya eating half the box before you realized they were stale? They must have been pretty good for "stale" doughnuts. Why not just bring back half of the next batch of "stale" doughnuts that you buy today."

So here I was with these useless doughnut holes and a couple of dollars less in my pocket. And what for? All because my sons were too impatient to wait for the soft, fresh doughnuts. They ate the hard, dry doughnut holes just because that was available for the moment. They missed out on my best for them because they refused to wait.

I couldn't help but feel sorry for them because they had eaten these hard, pastried golf balls. They wanted to be immediately satisfied even though it meant hard and dry.

My mind quickly drifted to how often we are too impatient to wait for the good things God has for us. So we just settle for less than God's best.

Don't be so quick to enter into another relationship. Don't be in such a hurry to take that new job or go into debt for a new purchase. Learn to wait for God and to wait on God no matter what it is. Let Him first show up and then you proceed to do things on His time table, not yours. You wouldn't want to forego the "fresh doughnuts" of life only to settle for what is stale, hard, and dry.

PRAYER REFLECTIONS AND NOTES

Then it came to pass, when Pharaoh had let the people go, that God did not lead them by way of the land of the Philistines, although that was near; for God said, "Lest perhaps the people change their minds when they see war, and return to Egypt." So God led the people around by way of the wilderness of the Red Sea. And the children of Israel went up in orderly ranks out of the land of Egypt. Exodus 13:17

Sometimes when God leads us out of our place of bondage, He doesn't lead us to our desired destination by way of the quickest possible route. We all of a sudden find ourselves free from slavery and wonder why we haven't immediately arrived at our glorious destination. Yes, we did finally come to a place where we are free, but perhaps we are not at a place where we can remain free. If we got to the promised land too soon, we'd only become enslaved there all over again. So God takes us by way of another route; the route that not only accommodates our present freedom, but also ensures our continued freedom. So that when we get to where we were meant to be in life, we'll be able to abide there.

God's desire for us is not just a delivered life, but a life of continual liberation. You may not like some of the roads that He leads you down. You may not be thrilled with His choice of scenery. But God always knows what is the best way for you to go.

This very moment, allow yourself to trust God. Allow yourself to be led by His hand down paths that you may not understand. Just know that when you look back over the journey, you'll be able to see how God really did know which roads were best for you to take.

We are hard-pressed on every side, yet not crushed; we are perplexed, but not in despair.   2 Corinthians 4:8

I once taught a study on diamonds for a class at my church. Diamonds have so many properties from which we can glean wisdom. Diamonds are rare and costly. They are the hardest natural substance known to man. Tons of earth must be dug and sifted through to find one diamond. But the diamond characteristic that I most likened to life was that in order for diamonds to produce the greatest possible brilliance, many little sides must be cut and then polished.

Sometimes in life we are cut on every side. There are things that happen to us that we wonder how we will make it through. Being separated or divorced is a major cut in our lives. It can make you feel like you will never recover.

I felt like life had lost all its luster. I believed I would never sparkle again. But thank God I was wrong. God brought me out of that dark place of despair, just as diamonds are brought up from deep within the earth. The places in my life that were cut, He gently hand-polished to bring out the greatest brilliance in me.

If you will place your wounded heart in the hands of God, the Master Jeweler, He will do the same for you. What God has allowed to happen to you was never meant to destroy you. He can use the things that you thought would crush you, to bring out the beauty that was hidden within.

I had not thought to see your face, but in fact, God has also shown me your offspring.
Genesis 48:11

𝒥acob had his beloved son, Joseph, torn away from him when Joseph was very young. Jacob was deceived by his other sons and made to believe that Joseph was dead. The Bible says that this so grieved Joseph that he refused to be comforted by anyone. He thought that he would go down to his grave with this grief. He never thought for one minute that he would ever see the one who was the apple of his eye and the delight of his soul. It had already been over twenty years since he had last seen Joseph. He never thought he would experience joy again. His mind couldn't even conceive of it.

Yet we read that Jacob not only saw Joseph, but he even got to see Joseph's children. He went on to live the life of a king with Joseph in Egypt for seventeen years.

At the end of his life, Jacob could hardly believe that not only was he able to look into the face of his beloved son, but he also beheld the generation after.

What in your life do you believe to be dead now? What have you lost all hope of ever having or seeing again? Have you come to believe that you will never know the depths of joy again? The sound of laughter ringing in your heart? Do you believe that you will never love again, the way you once loved?

Please take heart as you read the verse for today. Please be encouraged that you will experience all of these things again and more if you but open your heart to Jesus.

Do not focus on the pain of the moment, but believe with me that your experience will be as Jacob's was. God blessed him not only with what he longed to see, but far beyond that! And God can also do the same for you.

For she thought, "If I just touch His garments, I shall get well."
Mark 5:28 (NASB)

*I*f I can just touch Him. If I can just touch Him. I know I will be made well. This woman was desperate for wholeness. Internally she was bleeding. People were all around her, yet they could not see what was taking place within her. All those years of searching for a cure to the pain. Twelve years of blood loss. Blood is what gives us life, yet, she was steadily losing that which was life-giving. How she wanted healing for this affliction.

She turned to all of those who were supposed to know about healing and should have had the answers. But they had no answers. She pursued every avenue possible, but in the end she was worse off than when she started. She was bankrupt in every way. She had exhausted all alternatives and was left with a man she had only heard about; a man named Jesus.

After hearing what He had done for others, she was assured within herself that to touch Him was synonymous with being made whole. It didn't matter to her if He looked at her or laid hands on her. She knew that to be next to Him would bring what she needed most.

We can also have such faith. We can believe God and trust His loving heart. He loves us so much that even when His back is turned to us, His mercy will meet our needs. The faith of this woman met with the grace of God and produced healing. What could happen in your life today if you said to yourself, "If I can just touch Him."

For the Word of God is living and powerful and sharper than any two-edged sword, piercing even to the division of soul and spirit, and of joints and marrow, and is a discerner of the thoughts and intents of the heart. Hebrews 4:12

I have always loved the sciences and have been fascinated by medicine and how the body works. It is absolutely intriguing to me. I often read home remedy and herbal remedy books. I have tried many of them and been quite pleased with the results.

I remember one remedy in particular that I tried with my son. Against instruction, he had gone downstairs and sliced an apple with an extremely sharp knife. In the process, he cut his finger. He came upstairs screaming and dripping blood all the way. I tried applying pressure and that didn't work. I rinsed it with cold water and peroxide. That didn't work. I went through all of my motherly resources; none of which worked. So I prayed.

I asked God to help me figure out how to stop the bleeding. And immediately what came to mind was cayenne pepper. I ran downstairs to get it and apply it to this profusely bleeding cut. Almost upon contact, the bleeding stopped.

I wondered how the people in the home remedy book figured out that this stuff worked, but I was just grateful that someone came up with the idea.

I see the Word of God as cayenne pepper. There were times during my separation and divorce that my heart was profusely bleeding. I had tried everything I could think of to stop the bleeding. I had exhausted all of my resources when I finally asked God what I should do.

I found that God's Word is what heals my bleeding heart. It stops the bleeding upon contact. As soon as I begin to read, the healing instantaneously takes place. God seems to always lead me to a precise Scripture that relates to what I'm dealing with. Sometimes I might hear a sermon pertaining to that exact thing. But whatever way God chooses to get it to me, His Word always stops the bleeding.

Now yes, the cut is still there and I might still feel the hurt and pain at times. But the Words of Jesus bring inexplicable peace and healing to my heart.

Just like I ran to get the cayenne pepper, go ahead and run to the living and powerful Word of God. Apply it to your bleeding heart and watch it work on contact.

PRAYER REFLECTIONS AND NOTES

Now godliness with contentment is great gain. For we brought nothing into this world, and it is certain we can carry nothing out. And having food and clothing, with these we shall be content.
I Timothy 6: 6-8

We just celebrated Thanksgiving and I cannot help but to be filled with gratitude to God for all that He has brought my sons and me through.

As I prepared a feast for them and scheduled a weekend of fun for us, my heart was full of joy as I looked at their sweet, contented faces. I saw precious little young men around my candlelit table who were happy and just glad we had each other. Their tummies were stuffed, and God had seen to it that their hearts were too. They were longing for nothing nor lacked anything. Seeing that blessed my heart so much.

It could be so easy for them to crave something that someone else had or to want what they thought other families had, but they were perfectly content with us and what God had provided.

Watching them taught me a deep and spiritual lesson. I have often allowed myself to feel emptiness because I felt my life was missing something that someone else had. But this Thanksgiving, I looked at my little men, and I looked at my big God, and I experienced such deep satisfaction. My eyes were opened to the fact that I was surrounded by what I had always longed for and thought I never had. I was encompassed by not one, but three people who intently loved me and accepted me just as I am. Three people who wanted to be with me and to spend this wonderful day with just us.

My world stopped for just a moment to be truly grateful to God as I drank in this special moment in our lives. I could look toward the heavens and be thankful that I possessed that which mattered most.

Later that night, as we were all tucked away in bed, each son yelled from his room, "Happy Thanksgiving,

Mommy." Yes, indeed, it was a Happy Thanksgiving.

May our eyes continue to focus on all that we do have and not on what we don't. The "haves" far outweigh the "have-nots."

PRAYER REFLECTIONS AND NOTES

Then the men of Israel took some of their provisions; but they did not ask counsel of the Lord. So Joshua made peace with them and made a covenant with them to let them live; ... Joshua 9:14-15a

One year my sons and I decided that we would decorate our home well before Christmas. We actually began decorating before Thanksgiving. We wanted to fully enjoy the Christmas holidays for as long as possible before the New Year arrived. So here I was making it happen on the outside of the house with a 24-foot ladder. I had my 8 year-old son holding the ladder on one side and my 11 year-old son on the other. I tested all the lights we used from the year before. I wanted to make sure they all worked before I placed them all the way on the top. And they worked.

I clipped lights, taped lights, stretched lights, and did all that I could to attach the lights while not looking down, so I would not get dizzy.

Finally, as night was falling, we had finished our outside project. It was now time to turn the lights on. We plugged them in and they were just beautiful............all EXCEPT one side. Unfortunately, that one side of lights was almost at the highest point of the house. After all that hard work, I could have just kicked myself. I did not want to be at the highest point longer than needful and here I was having to climb that height again in an effort to troubleshoot.

The problem started when we ran out of the "tested" lights and opened a new pack without first inspecting them. We simply attached them to the house without a thought. Besides, they were new. All the old ones worked, so we just figured these new ones would surely work. To our great dismay, we were wrong at the highest point.

I began to think about how this is like finding a marriage partner or anything else we attach to our lives. We believe it will add light and beauty to us. Sometimes we thoroughly test many areas, yet we leave untested, the areas at the highest point that really matter most. Joshua and the Israelites discovered this too little, too late, when it came to the Gibeonites, all because they did not seek the Lord.

Let me encourage you to thoroughly test all areas of a person or a thing before you attach it to your life, especially the areas that will affect you at the highest and most crucial places. To test before attachment will cost you a lot less heartache than testing after you're already attached.

PRAYER REFLECTIONS AND NOTES

Why are you in despair, O my soul? And why are you disturbed within me? Hope in God, for I shall again praise Him; the help of my countenance, and my God.
Psalm 43:5

The words that I would use to describe my state of being at the beginning of my separation are despair, depression, and desperation. There seemed to be no way out and no one who understood. I was in such need of help and knew only one place to get it, and that was through prayer.

I was so "desperate" for prayer that I became a "prayer line junkie." You might feel that there is no way that you could get too much prayer, but I had surpassed the normal need and had gone into an act of compulsion.

Because I felt my friends didn't understand or I didn't want to burden them with my problems, I resorted to getting comfort from telephone prayer lines. I had about six to ten different ministries that I would call for prayer. I called them so often that I had their numbers memorized. I would call a prayer line in the morning to get me started for the day. I would call a prayer line at night to make sure I could sleep. Then I would call a prayer line in between if something happened that overwhelmed me. I called these prayer lines so much I just knew they had to recognize my voice. I thought about trying to deepen my voice or sound different so they wouldn't be on to me, but I really had to get my "prayer line fix."

Apparently, God had enough of me depending on the prayer lines and not coming to Him for myself so He came up with a plan to let me see that I had become a "prayer line junkie."

One day during my normal morning routine of calling the prayer line to get me started for the day, I called a well-known church prayer line. I told this particular prayer counselor ALL the things that were troubling me about my pending divorce, my concerns for my children, (who were at that time, 7 months old, 3 years old, and 6 years old) and whatever problems that related to my life at that time. I gave her all the information and sordid details so that she would know how to pray for me in my state of desperation.

Instead of this woman praying for me as I thought she would, she says to me with disbelief in an almost sing-song fashion and a very heavy Spanish accent, "What do you 'spect me to do? I think you need to go to a local pastor at a local church or something. But I don't really know what you 'spect me to do?" I said to her in an almost apologetic, stuttering manner, "Well, I- I was hoping, uhm, that you could pray for me." She said in a somewhat annoyed voice, "Well, okay, then, I will pray."

After I got off the phone with her, I laughed so hard that I fell off my bed. I was rolling on the floor, holding my stomach, I was laughing so hard. Every time I was tempted to become depressed, all I would have to do was think about this prayer line experience and I would laugh hysterically to the point of having tears in my eyes. That was years ago and I still get a good laugh out of it whenever I think of it.

God does not want us to be as those who are without hope. He wants our souls free of despair and depression. He will do whatever it takes to get you to come back to your old self. In my case, it took a prayer counselor with an accent and an attitude in San Antonio, Texas, to cure me of depression and of being a "prayer line junkie."

For I know the thoughts that I think toward you, says the Lord; thoughts of peace and not of evil, to give you a future and a hope. Jeremiah 29:11

One of the biggest lies that satan tells you is that the best of your life is now past. He tries to get you to believe that "what was" is as good as it is going to get. You start to feel that you have lived your best years and there is little to look forward to now that your ex-spouse will no longer be an intimate part of your life. Lies! These are nothing but lies. Let me assure you that your best years are yet to come if you place your life in God's hands.

I had started believing that I wouldn't have any friends like the close friends I had made while married. I thought my days of financial security, family vacations, and new experiences were over. I wondered if I would ever be able to make an impact on the world I lived in because I was divorced. All of these thoughts were concocted straight from whom God calls "the father of lies."

I can now look back over the past seven years and realize that none of those things were true. My life is filled with new friends, new adventures, and boundless opportunities. When we walk hand in hand with God, the future is not something to be dreaded, but something that we can excitedly look forward to because God has such good and hopeful things awaiting us.

He has made everything beautiful in its time.
Ecclesiastes 3:11a

One summer night some friends of mine renewed their wedding vows. It was such a lovely ceremony. They chose to have the ceremony in their backyard, which was simply beautiful. It looked like some kind of Eden with flowers, vegetation, benches, and a pond with fish. It was a wonderful and festive celebration kissed by a perfect summer night.

I could not help but reminisce about the last time I had seen their backyard. It did not look anything like it looked that summer night. There were some things that were growing, but there wasn't much that you would have called beautiful.

I figured they must have put a great deal of work into getting the yard to look like that. But my friend stated that they really hadn't done much more to the yard than had previously been done when I last saw it. The only difference was that the last time I came to their home, nothing was in bloom.

I was so amazed to think of what this yard had transformed into only by a change of seasons. When I thought about it, indeed it was in the winter when I had last visited their home. Just two seasons later, I really thought they must have worked their fingers to the bone to get results like this. But everything was already there. I just couldn't see it. The garden was just in its dormancy during the winter. Given a little time, it was metamorphosed into something alive and vibrant, bursting with magnificence and color.

The Lord brought to my mind how that was a picture of me. My life was once exuberant and full of life and laughter. But after divorce, I began going through a dormant and lifeless stage, where I questioned if I would ever be bursting with great joy and excitement again. I found myself wondering if that was going to be my permanent state of being.

But after seeing that garden, my hope was instantly renewed by this insight from God. All things have seasons of dormancy. All things have seasons that appear barren and lifeless. But just as fall changes the colors and winter strips the earth bare, spring and summer always follow these natural occurrences. What winter has taken away, spring WILL always replace. The earth will teem with new life again in the spring. Children will run with bare feet through the thick green grass of summer.

Though we might feel stripped of all life at times, we can be assured that it is only a season. We will live again, laugh again, and love deeply in life again. There is a newness and sweetness that awaits us. It will come. It can't help but to come because it is already within us. Now it is in a dormant state, but at least we can know that IT IS. It is there.

Winter can be cold, still, and solitary. But we can always endure it because we know in time, spring is coming and summer will follow. We must know this also about our lives. This lesson from nature should encourage our hearts to hope. So give it a little time. Solomon, who was known as the wisest man who ever lived, stated that God has made all things beautiful........ in His time.

Now both Jesus and His disciples were invited to the wedding. And when they ran out of wine, the mother of Jesus said to Him, "They have no wine." Jesus said to her, "Woman, what does your concern have to do with Me? My hour has not yet come." His mother said to the servants, "Whatever He says to you, do it." John 2:2-5

*J*ust a few nights ago, I was reading a Bible story to my sons, as is our bedtime ritual. We were reading about the first miracle that Jesus ever performed. He and His mother, Mary, were invited to a wedding. The custom at a wedding was to serve the good wine first, and then when everyone had partaken of a taste of the good stuff, then the second-rate wine would be served. At this particular wedding, the couple was about to be completely humiliated before all of their guests. They had not only used up all of the good wine, but the second-rate wine was all gone. The guests were still making merriment while waiting for the servants to bring out more wine; any wine. Then Jesus was told of this couple's predicament.

For some reason, I saw this story in a whole new light. I thought of having been married and having tried so hard to make my home a happy home. I read books, I attended seminars, I listened to tapes, and then tried to gather it all together and work it into my marriage and family. I adjusted, readjusted, and adjusted some more in hopes that I was doing all the things necessary to keep a husband happy and to have a successful family. But even with all of that effort, I could see that something was wrong. Realizing that all of my best wine was gone, I used whatever I had left of my "second-rate wine" to try to make life happier and more enjoyable for everyone. I felt like I was playing my part and my ex-husband's part, as well. I was taking care of my responsibilities and what had been his responsibilities just to ease whatever silent tension was slowly, but steadily building up. And even after offering the last drop of what little wine I had left, the guest of my marriage was still thirsty.

I can honestly say that I know what it is to have given marriage everything I had and then have to face the humiliation of having nothing left to offer. But what I love about this first miracle of Jesus is what He can do when there's nothing left.

Jesus got some empty vessels. Then, He requested that these vessels be filled with what was available; simple water. When the water that was poured into these vessels was tasted, it had turned into the very best wine that had been served all evening.

I do believe that during a separation and after a divorce, we face so much humiliation. We feel so very "used up." We are physically drained and emotionally depleted. We, too, are empty vessels needing to be filled. Yet Jesus looks at us, uses what we still have available, no matter how simple, and makes the inside of us better than anything that has been in us before.

After we yield ourselves to Him, and we do "whatever He tells us to" we also become full of the best "wine."

May we allow Jesus to perform this first of miracles in our lives. Instead of all of our best years being gone, may we look over our lives and be amazed that the best was truly saved for last.

COME AWAY WITH ME

My beloved spoke and said to me: "Rise up, my love, my fair one;

and come away.

For lo, the winter is past, the rain is over and gone. The flowers appear on the earth. The time of singing has come and the voice of the turtledove is heard in our land. The fig tree puts forth her green figs and the vines with the tender grapes give a good smell. Rise up, my love, my fair one;

And come away!

Song of Solomon 2:10-13

*PRAYER REFLECTIONS
AND
NOTES*

Contact Information

If you would like to contact Sonya P. Brundidge for speaking engagements or for information concerning publishing, books, or other products, please contact her by e-mail at:

simplyseasonspublish@myway.com

or write to:

Simply Seasons Publishing
P.O. Box 4110
Ft. Eustis, VA 23604